HOW TO SUCCEED AT GLOBALIZATION

HOW TO SUCCEED AT GLOBALIZATION

A Primer for Roadside Vendors

El Fisgón

Translated by Mark Fried

Metropolitan Books
Henry Holt and Company | New York

for Rocio

Metropolitan Books
Henry Holt and Company, LLC
Publishers since 1866
115 West 18th Street
New York, New York 10011

Metropolitan Books™ is a registered
trademark of Henry Holt and Company, LLC.

Originally published in Mexico in 2002 under the title
Hacia un despiporre global de excelencia y calidad
by Editorial Grijalbo (Grijalbo Mondadori), Miguel Hidalgo, Mexico.

Library of Congress Cataloging-in-Publication data
Barajas, Rafael.
   [Hacia un despiporre global de excelencia y calidad. English]
   How to succeed at globalization : a primer for roadside vendors /
El Fisgón ; translated by Mark Fried—1st American ed.
      p. cm
   ISBN 0-8050-7395-7
   1. International economic relations—History—Caricatures and car-
toons. 2. Globalization—Economic aspects—History—Caricatures and
cartoons. I. Title.

HF1359.B365 2004
337'.02'02—dc22   2003057034

Henry Holt books are available for special promotions and
premiums. For details contact: Director, Special Markets.

First American Edition 2004

Designed by Paula Russell Szafranski

Printed in the United States of America

10 9 8 7 6 5 4 3 2 1

CONTENTS

PROLOGUE

Let's face it: There's no way this book is going to make the bestseller list. To do that it would have to be yet another *How to Become a Millionaire*. And even though this text covers much of the same ground as your basic get-rich-quick guide, the sad truth is that this particular primer will only help you become even poorer than you were before you shelled out $15.00 to buy it. So the global sales prospects look pretty slim, since most of us are more interested in making a fortune than losing one, no matter what people say about misery loving company.

That's actually the first theory that needs debunking, because as you'll see, it's the companies that love misery. In these pages you will discover how the free market economy developed, from its humble origins in feudal days to its current stranglehold on the entire planet. We will examine how big businesses increase their profits through various degrees of exploitation, from the plunder of natural resources to the abuse of labor, from colonialism and war to monopolistic trade practices and planned layoffs.

How to Succeed at Globalization shows how the free market affects every aspect of our lives, including our self-esteem, our language, our identities. In the past you could be poor but respectable; today, if you're poor, you're just plain useless.

In recounting these developments, I have allowed myself the use of certain terms no longer in vogue, such as "capitalism," "imperialism," and "colonialism," because, vogue or no vogue, they're still the best labels around for certain contemporary phenomena—namely capitalism, imperialism, and colonialism. Similarly, Marxism—despite being a nineteenth-century philosophy—to this day remains a useful tool, especially for explaining the apparent paradox of how free markets turn so many into slaves.

Of course there are other words and concepts that more than adequately describe the behavior of modern-day multinational corporations. But overuse has dulled their edge. Rarely, then, does this book employ such terms as "corporate assholes," "greedy bastards," or "plutocratic sons of bitches." . . .

Happy reading.

INTRODUCING: CHARRO MACHORRO,
THE WORLD'S BIGGEST LOSER

SOMEWHERE IN THE GREAT SONORAN DESERT, A MAN CRAWLS THROUGH THE BURNING SANDS . . .

... DESPERATELY IN SEARCH OF ... WATER? SHADE? SHELTER FROM THE SCORCHING SUN?

OR MAYBE THIS POOR SUCKER'S STILL LOOKING FOR EL DORADO?

Nope. Don't need water. I got the Real Thing.

Nope. What I'm looking for is even better.

1

THREE DAYS EARLIER, THIS MAN SCALED A GIGANTIC WALL AND FOUGHT HIS WAY THROUGH DEADLY-SHARP BARBED WIRE.

HE SLIPPED PAST THE BORDER PATROL AND SET OUT NORTH THROUGH THE DESERT.

COULD HE BE A FUGITIVE, RUNNING FROM THE LAW?

WHAT DOES THIS MAN WANT?

Listen, there's no need to insult me. I'm an honest taxpayer.

Just a little career guidance. I want somebody to tell me how I can become the next Bill Gates.

THEN, OUT OF NOWHERE . . . AN OASIS . . . A CLINIC?

IT'S THE FAMOUS CASSANDRA CARRERA! FAITH HEALER, FINANCIAL SORCERESS, AND CAREER CONSULTANT.

Specialist in developing economies— I help losers get on their feet!

3

SERVING UP A MIX OF ANCESTRAL WISDOM AND NEW AGE SAVVY, CASSANDRA CARRERA'S CUTTING-EDGE CLINIC TREATS THIRD WORLD PEOPLE IN A SECOND-RATE CORNER OF THE FIRST WORLD.

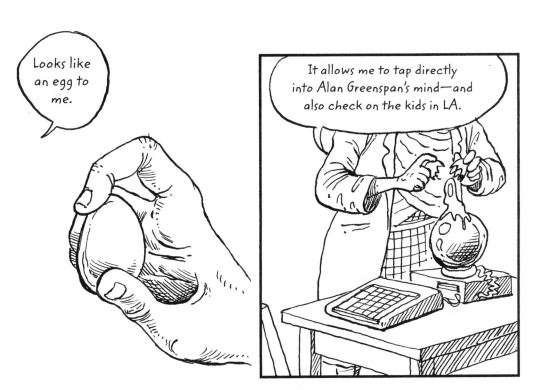

BACK IN THE MEDIEVAL PERIOD, ALL OF EUROPE LIVED UNDER FEUDALISM, A TOP-DOWN AUTHORITARIAN SYSTEM WHERE THE VAST MAJORITY OF PEOPLE LIVED IN POVERTY AND WERE COMPLETELY SUBJECT TO THE WHIMS OF KINGS AND NOBLES, WHO DID AS THEY ROYALLY PLEASED.

Drawing: Gustave Doré

THE FEUDAL LORD OWNED ALL THE LAND, WHICH WAS THE SINGLE MOST IMPORTANT SOURCE OF WEALTH.

THE PEASANTS, OR SERFS, WORKED THE LAND. THEY COULD KEEP A SMALL PART OF THE HARVEST, WHILE GIVING THE REST TO THE LORDS AND THE CHURCH.

THE OTHER MAJOR LANDHOLDER WAS THE CHURCH.

Engravings: Albrecht Dürer

A FEW PEOPLE LIVED OUTSIDE THE FEUDAL SYSTEM. MERCHANTS TRAVELED THE KNOWN WORLD SELLING THEIR WARES. AND NOW AND THEN A FEUDAL LORD WOULD FREE ONE OF HIS VASSALS, WHO'D PRACTICE A CRAFT OR OPEN A SHOP.

THE FIRST FREED SERFS WOULD SET UP THEIR SHOPS AT THE EDGE OF SETTLEMENTS AND TOWNS, IN THE BURGS OR BOROUGHS. THEY HIRED THE NEXT WAVE OF FREED SERFS TO WORK FOR THEM. AS TIME WENT ON, THE SHOP OWNERS SPENT LESS TIME WORKING AT THEIR TRADE AND MORE TIME MANAGING THEIR AFFAIRS. THIS WAS THE BEGINNING OF THE BOURGEOISIE.

Engravings: Albrecht Dürer

TO THE FEUDAL LORD, ALL WORLDLY GOODS DERIVED FROM GOD. TO THE NEW MERCHANT, THEY WERE COMMODITIES TO BE FREELY BOUGHT AND SOLD.

THE NEW MARKET ECONOMY WAS MORE EFFICIENT THAN THE FEUDAL ONE, AND THE MERCHANTS BEGAN TO ACCUMULATE WEALTH.

THE LANDED GENTRY, ON THE OTHER HAND, FOUND WORK DISTASTEFUL AND OFTEN LEFT THEIR LANDS UNTENDED.

Engravings: Albrecht Dürer

11

1. THE ENTREPRENEURS TAKE POWER

BY THE 17TH CENTURY, MORE AND MORE PEOPLE WERE REALIZING HOW UNFAIR IT WAS THAT THE GENTRY AND THE CLERGY GOT ALL THE GOODS BUT DID NONE OF THE WORK. AND PEOPLE BEGAN TO COMPLAIN.

IN 1649 THE ENGLISH PURITANS EXECUTED THEIR KING AND GOT RID OF THE MONARCHY FOR A FEW YEARS. A CENTURY AND A HALF LATER, THE FRENCH ROSE UP AND BEHEADED THEIR KING, THE QUEEN, AND SCORES OF ARISTOCRATS TO BOOT. AND GUESS WHO WAS BEHIND THE HEADCHOPPING? THE BANKERS, MANUFACTURERS, AND MERCHANTS.

Anonymous cartoon from the French Revolution

12

REVOLUTIONS IN AMERICA AND FRANCE AGAINST THE TYRANNY OF KINGS LED TO NEW FORMS OF GOVERNMENT IN WHICH ALL CITIZENS WERE EQUAL UNDER THE LAW. MAN WAS DECLARED TO HAVE BASIC INALIENABLE RIGHTS.

BUT THE SAME BOURGEOIS REVOLUTIONARIES SET UP AN ECONOMIC SYSTEM THAT WAS FAR FROM EQUAL, A SYSTEM THAT ALLOWED VERY FEW PEOPLE TO BECOME VERY RICH AT THE EXPENSE OF VERY MANY. THE SYSTEM IS CALLED CAPITALISM.

PEOPLE WERE SUPPOSED TO BE EQUAL UNDER THE LAW, BUT THE GAP BETWEEN RICH AND POOR MEANT THAT SOME WERE MORE EQUAL THAN OTHERS.

OVER THE COURSE OF THE 19TH CENTURY, EUROPE'S MONARCHIES LOST MORE AND MORE GROUND TO THE RISING MIDDLE CLASS. THE *ANCIEN RÉGIME* GAVE WAY TO THE NEW CAPITALIST ORDER.

The King is Dead! Long Live the Coin!

THE LAWS OF MONEY ARE CRYSTAL CLEAR.

In capitalism the only capital sin is to run out of capital.

And to keep from sinning, anything goes!

Engraving: Goya

2. THE INDUSTRIAL REVOLUTION AND THE SINS OF CAPITAL

THE ENTREPRENEURS GREW FAT AT THE EXPENSE OF EVERYONE ELSE AND SOON SWALLOWED UP SMALLER MARKETS, LOCAL ECONOMIES, AND COTTAGE INDUSTRIES.

THEY REALIZED THAT ALL WEALTH DEPENDS ON TWO THINGS:

THROUGHOUT HUMAN HISTORY, CLOTH HAD BEEN KNITTED BY HAND OR WOVEN ON HOME LOOMS. BUT DURING THE 18TH CENTURY, THE STEAM-POWERED LOOM WAS INTRODUCED IN ENGLAND, WHICH ALLOWED INDUSTRIALISTS TO PRODUCE TEXTILES ON A GRAND SCALE. OUT WENT HOMESPUN CLOTH; IN CAME THE TEXTILE MILL.

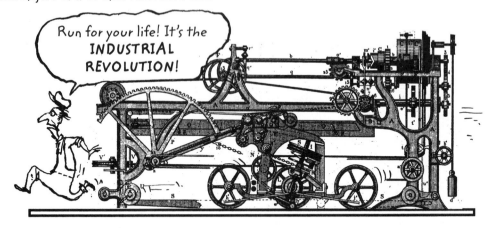

THE MOST BASIC LAW OF CAPITALISM IS THAT OF SUPPLY AND DEMAND.

THIS LAW SAYS THAT IF A LOT OF PEOPLE WANT A PARTICULAR PRODUCT, ITS PRICE WILL GO UP. AND IF THE PRODUCT IS IN SHORT SUPPLY, ITS PRICE WILL GO UP EVEN MORE. BUT IF THE MARKET IS FLOODED WITH A PRODUCT OR IF NOBODY WANTS IT, THE PRICE WILL FALL.

THE LAW OF SUPPLY AND DEMAND APPLIES AS MUCH TO LABOR AS TO GOODS.

Mechanization meant that industrialists no longer needed as many workers as they had before.

This created an army of unemployed people willing to work for next to nothing.

This in turn meant lower wages for those who had nothing to sell but their labor. Their families paid the price.

LARGE-SCALE UNEMPLOYMENT IS THE FOUNDATION OF BUSINESS WEALTH.

All us workers ever got out of the Industrial Revolution was an exhausting workday,

...subsistence wages,

...and a kick in the ass.

THE INDUSTRIALISTS STRUGGLED TO KEEP WAGES LOW AND PROFITS HIGH IN A WAR AGAINST THE WORKERS. TO DEFEND THEMSELVES AGAINST THE BOSSES' GREED, THE WORKERS FORMED UNIONS.

Hard as it is to believe, Charro, once upon a time unions actually defended the workers . . .

THE UNIONS SUCCEEDED IN WRESTING HISTORIC CONCESSIONS FROM THE BOSSES, LIKE THE EIGHT-HOUR WORKDAY, THE MINIMUM WAGE, THE RIGHT TO A PENSION, AND, IN SOME COUNTRIES, BENEFITS FOR THE UNEMPLOYED.

THE UNIONS BECAME THE BEST-ORGANIZED FORCE CHALLENGING THE CAPI-
TALISTS. FOR DECADES THEY PROVIDED A BASE FOR PARTIES THAT OPPOSED
GOVERNMENTS ALIGNED WITH BUSINESS INTERESTS. NATURALLY THE BOSSES
DID WHATEVER THEY COULD TO CORRUPT UNION LEADERS AND DIVIDE THE
WORKERS.

WHEN A FACTORY CLOSES OR WORKERS ARE LAID OFF, THE CAPITALISTS TRY TO
PIN THE BLAME ON THE UNIONS. BUT THE TRUTH IS THAT MANY MORE BANK-
RUPTCIES WERE CAUSED BY MARKET COMPETITION, SINCE BUSINESSES, TOO,
WERE SUBJECT TO THE IRON LAW OF SUPPLY AND DEMAND.

In the race to automate production, the most efficient companies crushed the competition. The winners gained control of the market, while the losers wound up on the street.

That hurt . . .

LITTLE BY LITTLE, SINGLE COMPANIES GAINED CONTROL OVER ENTIRE SECTORS OF THE ECONOMY, CREATING WHAT ARE KNOWN AS MONOPOLIES. MONOPOLIES HAD SO MUCH POWER THEY COULD TELL GOVERNMENTS WHAT TO DO, AND BRING THEM DOWN IF THEY REFUSED.

Do as I say—or else!

20

AT THE BEGINNING OF THE 19TH
CENTURY, THE BRITISH ECONOMIST
DAVID RICARDO DEVELOPED THE
THEORY OF ECONOMIC LIBERAL-
ISM, ACCORDING TO WHICH AN
UNREGULATED OR FREE MARKET IS
THE SOLUTION TO ALL PROBLEMS.
HE ALSO BELIEVED THAT FREE
TRADE AMONG NATIONS WOULD
BRING WEALTH AND PROSPERITY
TO ALL . . . AT LEAST IN THEORY.

Engraving: Gustave Doré and George Cruikshank

In practice the monopolies
grew to monstrous sizes and
crushed the smaller competition.

Meanwhile, the free market destroyed the
livelihoods of thousands of farmers, fish-
ermen, and craftsmen. The result: widespread hunger, disease, unrest. Chaos.

FRIGHTENED BY THE CONSEQUENCES OF A COMPLETELY UNBRIDLED MARKET ECONOMY,
GOVERNMENTS BEGAN TO REGULATE THE SYSTEM WITHIN THEIR TERRITORIES. BUT LITTLE
COULD BE DONE TO CONTROL THE AGGRESSIVE SPREAD OF CAPITALISM THROUGHOUT THE
WORLD.

THE INDUSTRIAL REVOLUTION WAS ACCOMPANIED BY A REVOLUTION IN TECHNOLOGY AS WELL. THE STEAM ENGINE WAS ADAPTED TO TRAINS AND SHIPS, WHICH MEANT CHEAPER, QUICKER, AND SAFER TRANSPORTATION. THE WORLD BEGAN TO SHRINK . . . FOR THOSE WHO HAD THE MEANS TO TRAVEL. THE REST WERE SIMPLY LEFT BEHIND.

Cartoon: George Cruikshank

THANKS TO THIS NEW TECHNOLOGY, THE 19TH-CENTURY MONOPOLISTS STEAMED FORTH INTO THE WORLD, CONQUERING MARKETS, RAW MATERIALS, AND CHEAP LABOR. IN THE PROCESS THEY TURNED LOCAL ECONOMIES INTO DUST.

3. COLONIALISM AND GLOBALIZATION IN THE AGE OF INDUSTRY

THERE'S NOTHING NEW ABOUT GLOBALIZATION. MANY SAY IT BEGAN WITH THE SPANISH CONQUEST. BUT WITH THE INDUSTRIAL REVOLUTION IT BECAME A LOT MORE VIOLENT.

IN THE EARLY DAYS, ALL IT TOOK WAS THE FREE MARKET TO BREAK DOWN BORDERS AND IMPOSE THE LAWS OF CAPITAL ON THE WORLD. WHEN THAT WASN'T ENOUGH, THERE WAS ALWAYS MILITARY FORCE.

THE WEALTHY INDUSTRIALIZED COUNTRIES BEGAN COMPETING FOR MARKETS AND RAW MATERIALS, SENDING THEIR ARMIES ALL ACROSS THE GLOBE. BY THE EARLY 20TH CENTURY, MUCH OF THE WORLD LAY UNDER THE CONTROL OF ENGLAND, FRANCE, BELGIUM, AND HOLLAND.

OVER TIME, THE CAPITALIST COUNTRIES BECAME MODERN COLONIAL EMPIRES.

THE OPIUM WARS ARE A PERFECT EXAMPLE OF CAPITALIST COLONIZATION: RUTHLESS, VIOLENT, AND COMPLETELY UNJUSTIFIED.

To balance their trade with China, the English illegally imported opium from India and sold it to the Chinese.

Bloody chink dope fiend!

When the Chinese government tried to stop this drug cartel, the British army invaded.

Bloody enemies of the free market!

BY IMPOSING CAPITALISM THROUGHOUT THEIR EMPIRES, THE COLONIAL POWERS DESTROYED LOCAL ECONOMIES THAT HAD SUSTAINED MUCH OF THE POPULATION, RESULTING IN:

ecological disasters,

famines and plagues,

mass emigration and death.

BEFORE THE FREE MARKET, EACH REGION WAS SELF-SUSTAINING, PRODUCING AND STORING ENOUGH GRAIN FOR ITS OWN CONSUMPTION.

IN THE NEW ECONOMY, FOOD, ESPECIALLY STAPLE GRAIN, BECAME A COMMODITY BOUGHT AND SOLD ON THE GLOBAL MARKET.

IN MANY PLACES, THE FARMERS COULDN'T COMPETE WITH BETTER, CHEAPER GRAIN FROM MORE FERTILE LANDS. IT BECAME CHEAPER TO BUY THAN TO PLANT.

THEN, IF THE PRICE OF GRAIN HAPPENED TO RISE, THEY COULD NO LONGER AFFORD TO BUY. MANY PEOPLE STARVED AS A RESULT.

DURING THE LAST DECADES OF THE 19TH CENTURY, AS MERCHANTS AND INDUS-
TRIALISTS IN A HANDFUL OF COUNTRIES AMASSED UNPRECEDENTED FOR-
TUNES, MANY OF THEIR COLONIES SUFFERED WAVES OF DROUGHT, FAMINE,
AND DISEASE, KILLING BETWEEN 30 AND 50 MILLION PEOPLE WORLDWIDE.

India: between 12 and 29 million dead

Brazil: about 2 million dead

China: between 19.5 and 30 million dead

Please—you're spoiling my appetite.

Drawing: S. Hernández

That's all jolly good, but those famines happened in the tropics, where the natives had always gone hungry.

But never on such a scale. And it was the free market that made things so much worse.

28

FREE MARKET PROSPERITY . . .

Hey, but don't forget, now we're free to set up roadside stands, and compete against the monopolies.

WORST OF ALL WAS THE FACT THAT THE STARVATION COULD HAVE BEEN AVOIDED.

IN ALMOST EVERY CASE, SURPLUS GRAIN WAS WITH-IN REACH OF THE STRICKEN REGIONS. BUT PEOPLE HAD NO MONEY TO BUY IT.

Period engraving

PEOPLE DIDN'T JUST CALMLY LIE DOWN AND DIE OF HUNGER, OF COURSE. ALMOST EVERY COLONY SAW SOME FORM OF ARMED REBELLION.

The famine of 1870 sparked hundreds of violent uprisings.

Then came the Boxer Rebellion in China.

The Extremist Revolt in India.

The Canudos War in Brazil.

All brutally suppressed.

Period engraving

THE CAPITALISTS TOOK ADVANTAGE OF EVERY NEW FAMINE AND EACH NEW WAVE OF REPRESSION TO ENLARGE THEIR EMPIRES.

Mind if I come in?

Cartoon: Honoré Daumier

4. A YOUNG WHEELER-DEALER NAMED SAM

THE YOUNGEST AND MOST DYNAMIC CAPITALIST COUNTRY WAS ITSELF ONCE A COLONY. WHEN THE UNITED STATES OF AMERICA DECLARED INDEPENDENCE FROM BRITAIN IN 1776, IT WAS SURROUNDED BY OTHER BRITISH, FRENCH, AND SPANISH COLONIES, BUT IT SOON CUT A DEAL WITH FRANCE AND SPAIN FOR THE NEARLY VIRGIN TERRITORIES OF LOUISIANA AND FLORIDA.

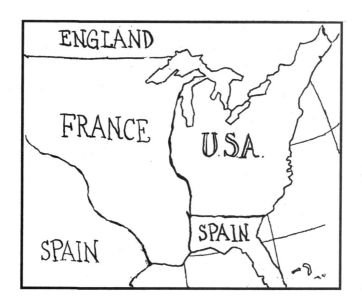

IN 1823, AFTER MEXICO AND THE REST OF LATIN AMERICA WON THEIR INDEPENDENCE FROM SPAIN, THE AMERICAN GOVERNMENT DECLARED THAT IT WOULD PROTECT THESE NATIONS FROM THREATS POSED BY EUROPEAN POWERS. THIS NEW POLICY BECAME KNOWN AS THE MONROE DOCTRINE. (APOLOGIES TO MARILYN)

THE U.S. SOON REALIZED THAT ITS NEIGHBORS HAD RICH RESOURCES, VIRTUALLY UNTOUCHED.

AND SO THE WEST WAS WON—BY KILLING OFF WHOLE TRIBES OF INDIANS AND WAGING AN UNJUST AND BLOODY WAR AGAINST MEXICO.

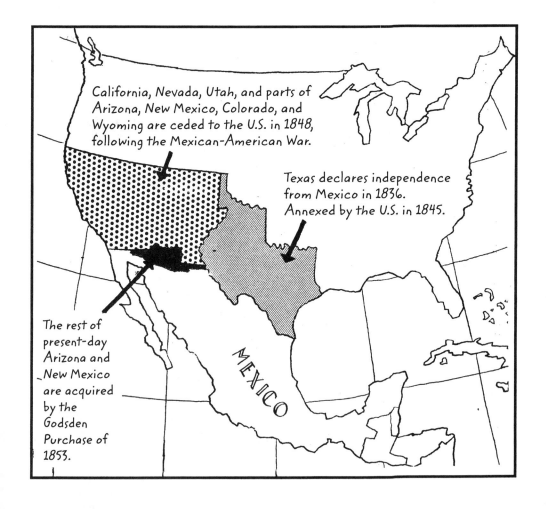

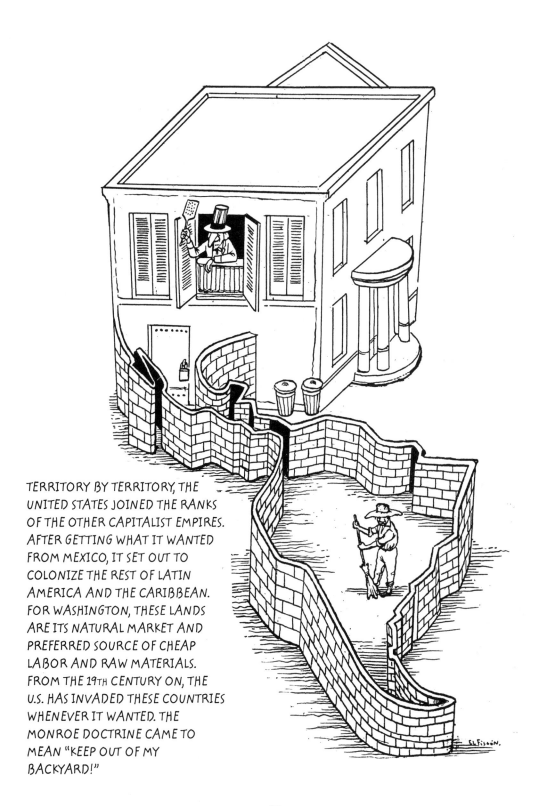

TERRITORY BY TERRITORY, THE
UNITED STATES JOINED THE RANKS
OF THE OTHER CAPITALIST EMPIRES.
AFTER GETTING WHAT IT WANTED
FROM MEXICO, IT SET OUT TO
COLONIZE THE REST OF LATIN
AMERICA AND THE CARIBBEAN.
FOR WASHINGTON, THESE LANDS
ARE ITS NATURAL MARKET AND
PREFERRED SOURCE OF CHEAP
LABOR AND RAW MATERIALS.
FROM THE 19TH CENTURY ON, THE
U.S. HAS INVADED THESE COUNTRIES
WHENEVER IT WANTED. THE
MONROE DOCTRINE CAME TO
MEAN "KEEP OUT OF MY
BACKYARD!"

THE UNITED STATES WAS QUICK TO GRASP THAT YOU DON'T HAVE TO OCCUPY A COUNTRY TO PLUNDER IT—CONTROLLING THE LOCAL ECONOMY DOES THE TRICK. OF COURSE, IT DOESN'T HURT TO HAVE A HUGELY POWERFUL ARMY.

JUST LIKE THE EUROPEAN EMPIRES, THE U.S. ACCUMULATED ENORMOUS WEALTH BY EXPLOITING ITS COLONIES, THEREBY DEVELOPING A THIRD WORLD OF ITS VERY OWN IN LATIN AMERICA.

THE WEALTH OF THE UNITED STATES IS THE POVERTY OF LATIN AMERICA.

5. WAR AND CAPITALISM (REDUNDANCY INTENDED)

THE COLONIZATION OF THE WORLD IN THE 19TH CENTURY DRAMATICALLY WIDENED THE GAP IN LIVING STANDARDS BETWEEN THE INDUSTRIALIZED NATIONS AND THEIR COLONIES.

HISTORIAN MIKE DAVIS UNDERSCORES THIS GROWING GAP AS EVIDENCE THAT WHAT WE KNOW TODAY AS THE THIRD WORLD CAME INTO BEING OVER A HUNDRED YEARS AGO.

THIS GLOBAL INEQUALITY IS MAINTAINED BY VIOLENCE. WAR IS PART AND PARCEL OF CAPITALISM, WHICH, AFTER ALL, WAS FORCED ON THE WORLD AT THE POINT OF BAYONETS. IN THE PROCESS, THE CAPITALISTS REALIZED THAT THERE'S NO BUSINESS LIKE WAR BUSINESS.

WAR IS ESPECIALLY GOOD FOR GETTING OUT OF A RECESSION. IT STIMULATES MANY SECTORS OF THE ECONOMY AND DEVELOPS NEW TECHNOLOGIES. AND WHAT BETTER WAY TO BEAT THE COMPETITION?

WAR AND VIOLENT EXPLOITATION KEEP THE MAJORITY OF PEOPLE IN MISERY, SO THAT A SMALL GROUP OF TYCOONS CAN LIVE IN LUXURY.

WHEN THE GREAT POWERS' PLANS FOR EXPANSION COLLIDE, THERE TENDS TO BE A BIG WAR. THE FREE MARKET IS RESPONSIBLE FOR A LOT OF WARS.

War is exactly like the free market: a ferocious contest with no holds barred.

Drawing: Honoré Daumier

IN 1914, GERMANY REALIZED IT HAD MISSED THE COLONIAL LANDGRAB, SO IT DECIDED TO ATTACK ITS NEIGHBORS. THIS LED TO A WAR OF SUCH UNPRECE-DENTED SCOPE IT WAS CALLED THE GREAT WAR. GERMANY, AUSTRO-HUNGARY, AND TURKEY ALLIED AGAINST FRANCE, ENGLAND, RUSSIA, AND THE UNITED STATES. (OF COURSE, THE WAR DIDN'T STAY UNPRECEDENTED, WHICH IS WHY IT'S NOW CALLED THE FIRST WORLD WAR.)

FROM 1914 TO 1918, THE WAR EMBROILED EVERY EMPIRE AND ITS COLONIES, WREAKING UNTOLD VIOLENCE AND DEVASTATION. IT ALSO TRIGGERED A REVOLUTION THAT THREATENED TO TOPPLE THE ENTIRE CAPITALIST SYSTEM.

HERE'S A BRIEF RECAP OF THE FIRST STAGE OF FREE TRADE EXPANSION.

1. Technological revolution (steam engine).

2. Exploitation of labor and massive unemployment.

3. Wars of conquest and economic colonialism.

4. Global restructuring of labor.

5. Plunder of indigenous economies and destruction of local communities. Social upheaval, violent unrest, popular resistance.

6. Cyclical economic crises.

7. Competition and conflict among the major capitalist powers, leading to world war.

41

6. SOCIALISM, NATIONALISM, AND RHEUMATISM

ORGANIZED RESISTANCE IS THE ONLY WAY TO BEAT THE MONEY MASTERS.

WORKERS FORMED LABOR UNIONS TO PROTECT THEMSELVES FROM EXPLOITATION.

OPPRESSED PEOPLES ROSE UP TO STOP THE PLUNDER OF THEIR NATURAL RESOURCES.

PEASANT REVOLTS AND NATIONAL UPRISINGS OCCURRED THROUGHOUT THE 19TH AND 20TH CENTURIES—ALL DIRECTED AGAINST THE OPPRESSION AND ECONOMIC DEVASTATION CAUSED BY THE EXPANDING CAPITALIST MONOPOLIES.

IN THE MID-19TH CENTURY, A MOVEMENT KNOWN AS SOCIALISM EMERGED WITH THE AIM OF PRESERVING HUMANIST VALUES IN THE FACE OF THE SAVAGERIES OF CAPITALISM.

THE MOST PROFOUND SOCIALIST THINKER WAS KARL MARX, WHO DISCOVERED THE LAWS THAT GOVERN CAPITALISM.

And to think they really believed we were serious about all that liberté, égalité, and fraternité.

Cartoon: Grandville (Jean Gerard)

I may be out of fashion these days, but nobody's done a better job explaining how capital makes the world go round.

THE SOCIALISTS ORGANIZED AND FORMED POLITICAL PARTIES. SINCE CAPITALISM, AS MARX HAD SHOWN, WAS ORGANIZED ON AN INTERNATIONAL SCALE, THE SOCIALISTS RESPONDED WITH A GLOBAL ORGANIZATION OF THEIR OWN: THE INTERNATIONAL WORKINGMAN'S ASSOCIATION.

Workers of the world, unite!

Or at least don't be so divided . . .

THE HORRORS OF CAPITALISM HELPED SPREAD THE MESSAGE OF SOCIALISM ACROSS THE GLOBE, BUT THE GOALS OF A SOCIALIST SOCIETY SEEMED A LONG WAY OFF . . . THEN, IN 1917, SMACK IN THE MIDDLE OF THE GREAT WAR, RUSSIAN REVOLUTIONARIES OVERTHREW THE GOVERNMENT AND ESTABLISHED THE UNION OF SOVIET SOCIALIST REPUBLICS, TRANSFORMING THE HISTORY OF THE 20TH CENTURY. CAPITALISTS ACROSS THE GLOBE SHUDDERED AS THEY REALIZED THAT IF THEY DIDN'T SHARE THE WEALTH, THEY RISKED BEING SWEPT OFF THE FACE OF THE EARTH.

SOCIALISM WAS THE GREATEST THREAT TO CAPITALIST DOMINATION, SO THE BUSINESS POWERS DECLARED WAR ON THE SOVIET UNION FROM THE START. WARS, INTERVENTIONS, TRADE EMBARGOES, AND SIMILAR ACTS OF AGGRESSION MADE IT IMPOSSIBLE FOR SOCIALISM TO DEVELOP.

And our biggest allies against socialism were . . . the Soviet bureaucrats.

BACK IN THE USSR, THE PARTY BUREAU-CRATS ACCUMULATED MORE AND MORE POWER AND PRO-MOTED A REGRESSIVE NATIONALIST MOVE-MENT. SOON THE COUNTRY BECAME A TOTALITARIAN DICTATORSHIP RULED BY JOSEF STALIN.

This dictatorship of the proletariat was a little over my head. That's why I settled for plain old dictatorship.

THE RUSSIAN REVOLUTION WASN'T THE ONLY THREAT TO THE COLONIAL POWERS TO COME OUT OF THE GREAT WAR. FIVE YEARS OF FIGHTING HAD WEAKENED THEIR IMPERIAL GRIP, AND NATIONALIST UPRISINGS BROKE OUT IN A NUMBER OF COLONIES.

Nationalism in the poor colonies is like nationalism in the powerful colonialist empires.

Historically, capitalist empires used nationalism as a pretext to justify colonial expansion.

In the colonies, however, nationalism helps people defend themselves against the great powers.

IN GENERAL, NATIONALIST MOVEMENTS IN COLONIZED COUNTRIES SOUGHT TO PROTECT PEOPLE'S LIVELIHOODS, TO ENSURE ADEQUATE FOOD, WATER, AND ENERGY, AND TO KEEP VITAL RESOURCES IN LOCAL HANDS.

7. THE SECOND WORLD WAR

THE GREAT WAR WROUGHT GREAT DESTRUCTION AND DISCORD. ENGLAND, FRANCE, AND THE USA DEFEATED GERMANY AND DIVVIED UP WHAT FEW COLONIES IT HAD.

THE GERMANS CONSIDERED THE TERMS OF SURRENDER HUMILIATING—AS FAR AS THEY WERE CONCERNED, THEY HADN'T BEEN DEFEATED. SO EVEN THOUGH ONE WAR WAS OVER, ANOTHER WAS CLEARLY IN THE OFFING.

AFTER THE END OF THE FIRST WORLD WAR, THE USA EMERGED AS THE LEADING CAPITALIST POWER. ITS ECONOMY GREW AT AN INCREDIBLE RATE OVER THE NEXT TEN YEARS.

IN FACT, THE BOOM WAS BUILT PRIMARILY ON SPECULATION, AND A CRISIS ENSUED IN 1929. THE STOCK MARKET CRASHED AND THE ECONOMY COLLAPSED.

THE CRISIS SPREAD ACROSS THE WORLD. IN GERMANY, INFLATION SOARED TO UNPRECEDENTED LEVELS. AS THE ECONOMIC SITUATION DETERIORATED, MORE AND MORE GERMANS SUPPORTED THE COMMUNISTS.

MANY ALSO SUPPORTED A PARTY CALLED THE NATIONAL SOCIALISTS, LED BY A CERTAIN ADOLF HITLER, WHOSE IDEAS WERE A HODGEPODGE OF NATIONALISM, RACISM, AND STATE CAPITALISM.

HIS SOLUTION TO THE CRISIS WAS TO BUILD A GREAT GERMAN EMPIRE.

MEANWHILE, BACK IN THE COLONIES, NEW NATIONALIST MOVEMENTS SPRANG UP.

IN THE U.S., PRESIDENT FRANKLIN D. ROOSEVELT TRIED TO REACTIVATE THE ECONOMY BY PROMOTING LARGE PUBLIC WORKS AND REGULATING CAPITALIST EXCESSES.

WHILE IN THE USSR, EVERYTHING SEEMED TO BE GOING EXACTLY ACCORDING TO (FIVE-YEAR) PLANS...

50

THE SOVIET UNION HAD BEEN THE GREAT HOPE OF SOCIALISM. BUT INSTEAD OF CREATING A COMMUNIST SOCIETY, STALIN'S PARTY BUREAUCRACY BUILT A TOTALITARIAN STATE THAT RULED BY TERROR.

STALIN ISOLATED HIS CHIEF OPPONENT, LEON TROTSKY, DIVIDED THE OLD-GUARD BOLSHEVIKS INTO OPPOSING CAMPS, AND THEN SET ABOUT ELIMI-NATING THEM ONE BY ONE.

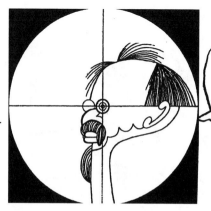

The apparatus of the workers' state has degenerated into a weapon of bureaucratic violence against the working class.

ON THE PRETEXT OF DEFENDING THE SOVIET UNION, STALIN UNDERCUT THE POWERFUL INTERNATIONAL SOCIALIST MOVEMENT AND ABANDONED MARXIST THEORY. (GROUCHO GOT MORE RESPECT THAN KARL.)

NEVERTHELESS, FEARFUL OF THE USSR AND REVOLUTIONARY MOVEMENTS, CAPITALIST GOVERNMENTS BEGAN MAKING SIGNIFICANT CONCESSIONS TO WORKERS, INCLUDING WAGE HIKES, PENSIONS, HEALTH PLANS, AND EDUCATION.

IN EUROPE, CONFLICTS AMONG THE CAPITALISTS BECAME INCREASINGLY SEVERE. IN SPAIN, A GROUP OF FASCIST ARMY OFFICERS REBELLED AGAINST THE REPUBLIC IN 1936, PLUNGING THE COUNTRY INTO A BLOODY CIVIL WAR. AND IN 1939, GERMANY INVADED POLAND AND SET OFF THE SECOND WORLD WAR.

OF COURSE, THE BIG WEAPONS MANUFACTURERS MADE A HUGE KILLING.

THE SECOND WORLD WAR SUBSTANTIALLY EXPANDED THE GLOBAL CATA-
LOGUE OF HORRORS, MOSTLY THANKS TO GERMAN, JAPANESE, AND ITALIAN
FASCISM.

BLITZKRIEG.

BOMBING OF CIVILIANS.

TORTURE AND TERROR.

CONCENTRATION CAMPS.

HOLOCAUST AND
GENOCIDE.

AND THE ATOMIC BOMB,
WHICH THE U.S. DROPPED ON
HIROSHIMA AND NAGASAKI.

8. SOME BURNING ISSUES OF THE COLD WAR

IN THE AFTERMATH OF THE SECOND WORLD WAR, COMMUNISTS TOOK OVER IN CHINA, WHILE GOVERNMENTS THAT CLAIMED TO BE SOCIALIST WERE SET UP IN EASTERN EUROPE.

SO THE NEW WORLD ORDER HAD TWO LARGE BLOCS: THE "FREE WORLD" LED BY THE USA, AND THE "SOCIALIST BLOC" LED BY THE USSR.

THE TWO SUPERPOWERS LAUNCHED AN ARMS RACE THAT BROUGHT THE WORLD TO THE BRINK OF EXTINCTION AS THEY DEVELOPED AND STOCKPILED MORE AND MORE POWERFUL BOMBS. IN THOSE DAYS, THINKING BIG MEANT THINKING *KABOOM*.

TO KEEP UP IN THE ARMS RACE, THE USSR NEGLECTED OTHER VITAL SECTORS OF THE ECONOMY, WHILE IN THE CAPITALIST WORLD THE ARMS INDUSTRY ONCE AGAIN HELPED FUEL THE ENTIRE ECONOMY.

SOON AFTER THE SECOND WORLD WAR, A WAVE OF REVOLUTIONS (IN CHINA, INDIA, AND ELSEWHERE) BROKE UP EUROPE'S COLONIAL EMPIRES, GIVING RISE TO NEW NATION-STATES ACROSS THE GLOBE.

NEARLY ALL OF THESE NEW COUNTRIES SOUGHT TO CONTROL CRUCIAL SECTORS OF THEIR NATIONAL ECONOMIES, LIKE ENERGY, TRANS-PORTATION, AND COM-MUNICATIONS. THEY SET UP STATE COMPANIES TO DEFEND THEIR RESOURCES FROM THE LARGE MULTINATIONALS.

Just like Lázaro Cárdenas did in Mexico when he nationalized the oil industry!

THESE MEASURES SERVED TO CHECK THE VORACITY OF BIG BUSINESS. MANY COUNTRIES EVEN WENT SO FAR AS TO SET UP WELFARE STATES THAT—OH, MY GOD!—REGULATED THE ECONOMY AND SHARED THE WEALTH.

The lives of millions throughout the world were noticeably improved.

And the destruction of local economies was slowed.

BUT AS THE YEARS WENT BY, EVEN THESE WELFARE STATES BOUGHT INTO THE LOGIC OF CAPITALISM . . .

ACCORDING TO WASHINGTON, THE OBJECTIVE OF THE COLD WAR WAS TO DEFEND FREEDOM (OF BUSINESS) AND DEMOCRACY (FOR BUSINESSMEN) AGAINST COMMUNISM.

BUT THAT DOESN'T EXPLAIN WHY THE U.S. OVERTHREW NATIONALIST LEADERS WHO WEREN'T COMMUNIST, SUCH AS ARBENZ IN GUATEMALA, MOSSADEGH IN IRAN, PERÓN IN ARGENTINA, SUKARNO IN INDONESIA, GETÚLIO VARGAS IN BRAZIL, LUMUMBA IN THE CONGO, AND MANY OTHERS.

OR WHY THEY SLAPPED A TRADE EMBARGO ON CUBA AFTER THE REVOLUTION IN 1959. IT WAS ACTUALLY U.S. BELLIGERENCE THAT PUSHED CASTRO INTO THE ARMS OF THE SOVIETS.

59

IN FACT, THE COLD WAR WAS A CRUSADE LED BY THE UNITED STATES AGAINST BOTH SOCIALIST AND NATIONALIST INFIDELS, WITH THE ULTIMATE GOAL OF CONVERTING THE WHOLE WORLD TO CAPITALISM.

CONSEQUENTLY, MANY OF WASHINGTON'S INTERVENTIONS WERE TO DEFEND THE INTERESTS OF THE U.S. CORPORATIONS THAT WANTED IRAN'S OIL, CHILE'S COPPER, GUATEMALA'S BANANAS . . . AND ON AND ON.

THE INTERVENTIONS RANGED FROM INVASIONS TO ASSASSINATIONS OR OTHER COVERT ACTS. IN THE U.S.'S OWN HEMISPHERE, THE LIST OF TARGETED COUNTRIES GREW LONGER AND LONGER:

CUBA, NICARAGUA, GUATEMALA, PUERTO RICO, HONDURAS, COSTA RICA, EL SALVADOR, THE DOMINICAN REPUBLIC, PANAMA, COLOMBIA, PERU, VENEZUELA, BRAZIL, BOLIVIA, PARAGUAY, CHILE, ARGENTINA, URUGUAY, GRENADA, VIRGIN ISLANDS . . .

BUT THE U.S. ALSO "PROTECTED ITS INTERESTS" IN ASIA AND AFRICA, INTER-VENING IN: KOREA, VIETNAM, CAMBODIA, THE PHILIPPINES, SAUDI ARABIA, IRAQ, IRAN, AFGHANISTAN, JORDAN, LEBANON, SYRIA, THAILAND, ALGERIA, EGYPT, ETHIOPIA, SOMALIA, INDONESIA, PALESTINE, CONGO . . .

ONE OF THE MOST VIOLENT ENCOUNTERS BETWEEN THE "FREE WORLD" AND THE "SOCIALIST BLOC" TOOK PLACE IN THE SMALL SOUTHEAST ASIAN COUNTRY OF VIETNAM, WHERE THE USA FOCUSED ALL ITS MILITARY MIGHT ON LOCAL COMMUNIST INSURGENTS—MOSTLY SIMPLE PEASANTS—AND LOST.

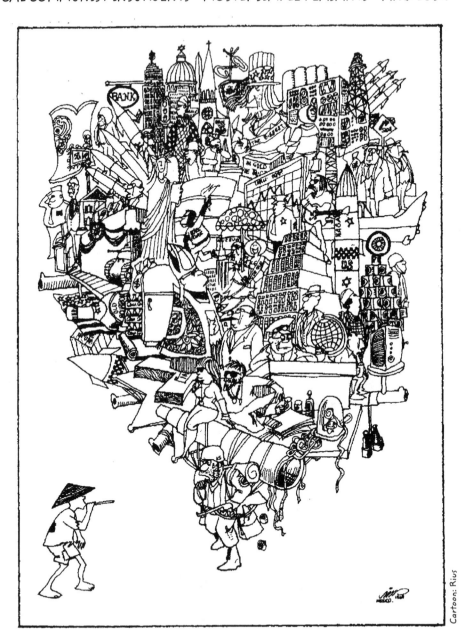

Cartoon: Rius

IN AN EXTRAORDINARY AND MOVING DISPLAY OF CIVIC RESPONSIBILITY, THE PEOPLE OF THE UNITED STATES TOOK TO THE STREETS IN PROTEST TO DEMAND THAT THE TROOPS BE PULLED OUT OF VIETNAM—AND WON.

THOUGH THEY CLAIMED IT WAS ALL TO DEFEND THE FREE WORLD (AGAINST COMMUNIST DESPOTISM, OF COURSE), WASHINGTON SUPPORTED BRUTAL DICTATORS GUILTY OF THE WORST HUMAN RIGHTS VIOLATIONS: SOMOZA, TRUJILLO, DUVALIER, CASTILLO ARMAS, BANZER, STROESSNER, FERDINAND MARCOS, IDI AMIN DADA, PINOCHET, VIDELA, THE SALVADORAN JUNTA, THE BRAZILIAN COLONELS . . .

HAVING LONG ABANDONED THE IDEA OF INTERNATIONAL SOCIALIST REVOLUTION, THE USSR WAGED A WAR OF STRATEGIC POSITIONING, BACKING REVOLUTIONARY MOVEMENTS WHEN THESE SQUARED WITH SOVIET INTERESTS, AND CUTTING OFF SUPPORT WHEN THEY DIDN'T.

63

SOCIALISM AS PRACTICED MOVED FURTHER AND FURTHER AWAY FROM SOCIALIST IDEALS, SO THAT THE SOVIET BLOC OFFERED NO HUMANIST ALTERNATIVE TO THE VIOLENCE OF CAPITALISM. WITH NO FREEDOM OF EXPRESSION OR REAL DEMOCRACY, "SOCIALIST" COUNTRIES FROM CUBA TO CHINA DEVELOPED REPRESSIVE AND INEFFICIENT STALINIST BUREAUCRACIES.

THE DEGENERATION OF THE WORKERS' STATES LED TO TRULY DEGENERATE IDEAS. IN CAMBODIA, WHERE THE U.S. HAD COMMITTED SERIOUS WAR CRIMES, THE ULTRA-LEFT KHMER ROUGE TOOK POWER AND PROCEEDED TO MURDER MILLIONS OF PEOPLE—ALL IN THE NAME OF SOCIALISM.

Engraving: Gustave Doré

IN THE EARLY 1970s, THE WORLD ECONOMY TOOK A DOWNSWING. CAPITALIST COUNTRIES SUFFERED STAGNATION AND INFLATION AT THE SAME TIME. TAX REVENUES FELL WHILE SOCIAL NEEDS SOARED. THE BUSINESSMEN HAD A SIMPLE ANSWER: THE FREE MARKET. THE LESS GOVERNMENT REGULATION AND REDISTRIBUTION, THE BETTER (FOR THE BUSINESSMEN, OF COURSE).

THIS RESURGENCE OF ECONOMIC LIBERALISM SIGNALED THE RETURN OF UNBRIDLED CAPITALISM, KNOWN AS NEOLIBERALISM.

9. HOW NEO IS NEOLIBERALISM?

NEOLIBERALISM EMERGED AFTER THE SECOND WORLD WAR AS A REACTION AGAINST THE REGULATED ECONOMY OF THE WELFARE STATE.

THE NEOLIBERALS REVIVED THE ECONOMIC LIBERALISM ESPOUSED BY DAVID RICARDO IN THE EARLY 19TH CENTURY. FOR THEM, FREE ENTERPRISE IS THE ONLY SOURCE OF WEALTH AND THE SOLUTION TO ALL ECONOMIC WOES.

NEOLIBERALS WANT TO ELIMINATE OR SHRINK THE STATE AS MUCH AS POSSIBLE. THEY BELIEVE THAT FREEDOM AND PROGRESS CAN COME ONLY FROM A FREE MARKET AND OPEN COMPETITION.

THE LAW OF THE FREE MARKET IS THE LAW OF THE JUNGLE: ECONOMIC DARWINISM. IN THE FOOD CHAIN OF CAPITAL, THE BIG FISH ALWAYS EAT THE LITTLE FISH, WHICH IS GREAT IF YOU'RE A BIG FISH BUT NOT SO HOT IF YOU'RE WHAT'S FOR DINNER.

BUT RICARDO NEVER COULD HAVE IMAGINED HOW BIG AND VORACIOUS THE MULTINATIONAL CORPORATIONS WOULD BECOME. NOTHING AND NO ONE COULD COMPETE WITH THEM. AND THAT WAS SOMETHING ENTIRELY NEO.

UNTIL THE 1970s, HOWEVER, THE NEOLIBERALS WERE TOO SCARED TO PUT THEIR THEORIES INTO PRACTICE—FOR FEAR THE PEOPLE MIGHT TAKE TO THE STREETS. AT FIRST, ONLY CHILEAN DICTATOR AUGUSTO PINOCHET DARED APPLY THEM—AFTER HE'D EXTERMINATED ALL POSSIBLE OPPOSITION. FOR SAVAGE CAPITALISM, YOU NEED A SAVAGE DICTATOR.

EL FISGÓN.

A 1989 STUDY FOUND THAT THE NUMBER OF POOR PEOPLE IN CHILE ROSE FROM ONE MILLION TO SEVEN MILLION AS A RESULT OF PINOCHET'S NEOLIBERAL POLICIES. BUT THE EXPERIMENT WAS A GRAND SUCCESS FOR THE WEALTHY, SO IT WAS SOON TRIED IN OTHER PARTS OF THE WORLD.

IN 1979, MARGARET THATCHER TOOK OVER IN GREAT BRITAIN; A YEAR LATER RONALD REAGAN WAS ELECTED PRESIDENT IN THE U.S. UNABASHEDLY PROMOTING THE INTERESTS OF BIG BUSINESS, THEY BECAME THE POLITICAL PARENTS OF NEOLIBERALISM AND SPAWNED A NUMBER OF CHILDREN WHO WERE TRULY BASTARDS.

AS WE HAVE SEEN, THE CAPITALISTS ALWAYS SEEK TO DRIVE DOWN THE COSTS OF LABOR AND RAW MATERIALS. SO THE FIRST CAMPAIGN LAUNCHED BY THE NEOLIBERALS WAS AGAINST ORGANIZED LABOR.

THATCHER AND REAGAN LED THE CHARGE AGAINST THE UNIONS AND CRUSHED AS MANY STRIKES AS THEY COULD.

THE FIRST WAVE OF ATTACKS WAS MADE POSSIBLE BY A NEW TECHNOLOGY THAT WAS EVERY BIT AS INFLUENTIAL AS THE STEAM ENGINE: THE MICRO-PROCESSOR. AND SO THE COMPUTER REVOLUTION WAS UNDER WAY.

10. THE COMPUTER REVOLUTION

COMPUTERS MADE WORKERS FAR MORE PRODUCTIVE.

ALL THE COMPANIES STARTED USING COMPUTERS ... AND LAYING OFF WORKERS.

SOON THE BOSSES REALIZED HOW COMPUTERS COULD HELP THEM CUT COSTS ... AND WORKERS.

THE UNIONS COLLAPSED. A WHOLE GENERATION OF WORKERS WAS LEFT DEFENSELESS.

THE REVOLUTION IN COMPUTER TECHNOLOGY BROUGHT ABOUT CHANGES VERY SIMILAR TO THOSE SEEN DURING THE INDUSTRIAL REVOLUTION.

JUST LIKE IN THE 18TH AND 19TH CENTURIES, BOSSES USED THE TECHNOLOGICAL CHANGES TO SACK SOME WORKERS AND LOWER THE WAGES OF THE REST.

THE TECHNOLOGICAL REVOLUTION ALLOWED THE BIG MONOPOLIES TO REORGANIZE THEIR PRODUCTION AND RESTRUCTURE THEIR WORKFORCE ON A GLOBAL SCALE.

THANKS TO COMPUTERS, BIG COMMERCIAL BANKS CAN TRANSFER MILLIONS OF DOLLARS IN SECONDS AND COMPANIES CAN CONDUCT GLOBAL TRANSACTIONS AT THE CLICK OF A BUTTON. A TRADER IN NEW YORK CAN BUY COTTON IN CHINA, HAVE THE CLOTHES SEWN IN HAITI, AND SELL THE FINISHED PRODUCT IN EUROPE. THE WHOLE WORLD HAS BEEN LINKED UP INTO ONE GIANT ECONOMY.

THIS UNREGULATED GLOBAL MARKET IS SO EFFICIENT THAT NO LOCAL ECONOMY CAN COMPETE. WHAT'S MORE, SOME LOCALES JUST AREN'T OF ANY INTEREST TO THE MARKET.

WIDE SWATHS OF AFRICA AND LATIN AMERICA WERE BUFFETED BY GLOBALIZATION AND THEN EXCLUDED FROM IT.

BUT IT WAS A DIFFERENT STORY FOR THE BIG BANKS AND MONOPOLIES. THEY WERE NOW IN A POSITION TO RUN THE WORLD'S ECONOMY TO SUIT THEIR OWN INTERESTS.

PEOPLE SAY GLOBALIZATION HAS REALLY SHRUNK THE PLANET, AND THEY'RE RIGHT—AT LEAST AS FAR AS THE WEALTHY ARE CONCERNED. WHAT SHRANK FOR THE WORKERS WAS THEIR PROSPECTS. WHILE THE MASTERS OF MONEY CAN ZIP AROUND THE WORLD AS THEY PLEASE, WORKERS AND THEIR UNIONS HAVE TO FIGHT IT OUT AT HOME.

MEANWHILE THE REORGANIZATION CONTINUED, WITH COMPANIES RELOCATING THEIR FACTORIES WHEREVER LABOR WAS CHEAPEST, DEPRESSING WAGES WORLD-WIDE AND DEMOLISHING UNIONS.

A NEW GLOBAL CAMPAIGN WAS LAUNCHED THAT SOUGHT TO DO AWAY WITH EVERYTHING THE WORKERS' MOVEMENT HAD ACHIEVED: THE EIGHT-HOUR DAY, MINIMUM WAGE, HEALTH AND PENSION PLANS.

THE MULTINATIONAL CORPORATIONS ARE SO ENORMOUSLY POWERFUL IN THE USA THAT THEY CAN TELL THE GOVERNMENT WHAT TO DO. IN WASHINGTON, IT'S GOVERNMENT BY THE MULTINATIONALS, FOR THE MULTINATIONALS.

THE ECONOMIC CLOUT OF THESE MEGA-COMPANIES IS OFTEN GREATER THAN THAT OF THE COUNTRIES IN WHICH THEY OPERATE. THEY CAN SINK EVEN MIDSIZED ECONOMIES IN A MATTER OF HOURS.

11. HOW TO IMPOSE NEOLIBERALISM

FOR DECADES, THE WELFARE STATES OF THE DEVELOPING WORLD ENJOYED A HEALTHY AVERAGE GROWTH RATE OF 6 PERCENT A YEAR. BUT WHEN THE CRUNCH HIT IN THE 1970s, WASHINGTON AND THE INTERNATIONAL FINANCIAL INSTITUTIONS MOVED TO IMPOSE THE NEOLIBERAL SYSTEM ON THE THIRD WORLD.

THIS NEW OFFENSIVE WAS OFFENSIVE IN MORE WAYS THAN ONE. THERE WAS POLITICAL PRESSURE, ECONOMIC HARASSMENT, MILITARY INTERVENTION ... AND IT ALL BEGAN WITH SOMETHING CALLED THE FOREIGN DEBT.

IN 1972, THE U.S. ECONOMY WAS IN RECESSION, SO WASHINGTON AND BUSINESS HATCHED A PLAN TO REVIVE IT. THEY LOBBIED AND BRIBED TO PUSH CHEAP LOANS ONTO VARIOUS THIRD WORLD GOVERNMENTS SO THAT THESE COUNTRIES WOULD BUY THINGS ON CREDIT FROM U.S. COMPANIES. AT FIRST THE INTEREST RATES WERE LOW, BUT AS THE U.S. ECONOMY PICKED UP, SO DID THE RATES, AND THE DEBTS SOON BECAME UNPAYABLE.

THE HISTORY OF THE DEBT THE THIRD WORLD NEVER WANTED IS A STORY OF HUMILIATION AND BETRAYAL, TREASON, AND GRAFT BEYOND BELIEF.

FOR LATIN AMERICA, THE DEBT HAS BEEN LIKE AN OPEN WOUND AND SEVERAL COUNTRIES HAVE GONE INTO SHOCK. THE OBVIOUS WAY OUT WAS SIMPLY NOT TO PAY, AND IN 1982, THERE WAS TALK OF A JOINT MORATORIUM ON DEBT PAYMENTS BY THE THREE LARGEST LATIN AMERICAN DEBTORS: MEXICO, BRAZIL, AND ARGENTINA.

HAD THE MAJOR DEBTORS DEFAULTED, THE GLOBAL FINANCIAL SYSTEM MIGHT HAVE COLLAPSED, AND THE BANKS WOULD HAVE HAD TO SETTLE FOR SUBSTANTIAL REDUCTIONS IN PAYMENT. THAT WOULD HAVE MEANT A SIGNIFICANT LOSS OF REVENUE FOR THE U.S.

WASHINGTON THREATENED AND BULLIED AND MANAGED TO DIVIDE THE LATIN AMERICAN GOVERNMENTS. THE BANKS OFFERED BRIDGE LOANS THAT ONLY INCREASED THE SIZE AND TERM OF THE DEBT AND MADE IT LESS POSSIBLE TO PAY. AND, FOR GOOD MEASURE, THEY RAISED THE INTEREST RATES.

IN 1986 THE SITUATION IN PERU BECAME CRITICAL. PRESIDENT ALÁN GARCIA DECLARED HE WOULD ALLOCATE NO MORE THAN 10 PERCENT OF THE COUNTRY'S EXPORT EARNINGS TO PAY THE DEBT. TO KEEP OTHERS FROM FOLLOWING SUIT, THE U.S. AND THE BIG BANKS BOYCOTTED PERU AND DROVE ITS ECONOMY INTO THE GROUND.

THE INTERNATIONAL MONETARY FUND (IMF) WAS ORIGINALLY DESIGNED TO RESCUE COUNTRIES TEMPORARILY STRAPPED FOR CASH, BUT IT WOUND UP BECOMING A COLLECTION AGENCY FOR THE BIG BANKS. IT INTERVENED IN THE DOMESTIC AFFAIRS OF POOR COUNTRIES, DICTATING ITS WILL IN SO-CALLED LETTERS OF INTENTION (AND THEIR INTENTIONS WERE FAR FROM GOOD).

NEOLIBERAL PROPAGANDA INSISTED THAT FREE COMPETITION AND ECONOMIC MODERNIZATION WOULD PULL THE THIRD WORLD OUT OF ITS BACKWARD, UNDERDEVELOPED STATE— BUT THE CASE WASN'T VERY CONVINCING.

NEOLIBERALISM WAS PROMOTED IN THE THIRD WORLD BY THE LOCAL PARTNERS OF THE MULTINATIONAL CORPORATIONS AND BY GOVERNMENT OFFICIALS WHO MADE CAREERS OUT OF NEGOTIATING WITH INSTITUTIONS LIKE THE IMF.

A FEW LATIN AMERICAN NEOLIBERALS RODE WASHINGTON'S COAT-TAILS TO POWER IN THEIR OWN COUNTRIES: MENEM IN ARGENTINA, SALINAS AND ZEDILLO IN MEXICO, AND TOLEDO IN PERU— ALL FINE SPECIMENS OF NEO-BASTARDS.

THE NEOLIBERAL PROGRAM WAS IMPOSED ON LATIN AMERICA WITH THE HELP OF CORRUPT, AUTHORITARIAN REGIMES. AND WASHINGTON BROOKED NO RESISTANCE, EVEN IF IT MEANT RESORTING TO VIOLENCE. SUCH WAS THE CASE WITH PANAMA, WHEN STRONGMAN MANUEL NORIEGA PLAYED A STRATEGIC CARD: THE PANAMA CANAL.

FIRST THE U.S. APPLIED ECONOMIC PRESSURE, AND THEN REAGAN'S SUCCESSOR, GEORGE BUSH, SENIOR, ACCUSED NORIEGA (WHO HAD BEEN A CIA STOOGE AND A CLIENT OF WASHINGTON FOR YEARS) OF DRUG TRAFFICKING. THE U.S. INVASION, "OPERATION JUST CAUSE," WAS LAUNCHED AGAINST PANAMA ON DECEMBER 19, 1989.

WASHINGTON TOOK THIS OPPORTUNITY TO TEST ITS NEW STATE-OF-THE-ART "STEALTH" TECHNOLOGY AGAINST AN UNARMED OPPONENT. PANAMA BECAME A LABORATORY OF HORROR.

TO DIFFUSE ANY ADVERSE REACTIONS, WASHINGTON CARRIED OUT AN EFFECTIVE DISINFORMATION CAMPAIGN, CLAIMING THAT THE PANAMANIANS SUPPORTED THE INVASION, WHILE DOWNPLAYING THE NUMBER KILLED, WHICH, AS WE KNOW TODAY, WAS NEARLY FIVE THOUSAND.

12. WORLD-CLASS PLUNDER

AFTER THE RESTRUCTURING OF THE FOREIGN DEBT, THE DE-STRUCTURING OF THE PERUVIAN ECONOMY, AND THE INVASION OF PANAMA, OTHER NATIONS IN THE REGION HAD LITTLE CHOICE BUT TO EMBRACE THE POLICIES OF NEOLIBERALISM. ALL VOLUNTARILY, OF COURSE—AT GUNPOINT.

ACCORDING TO THE NEOLIBERAL POLICYMAKERS, IF A FREE-MARKET ECONOMY DOESN'T SHOW SIGNS OF GROWTH, IT'S JUST NOT COMPETING HARD ENOUGH.

THEY CLAIMED THAT NATIONALIST, POPULIST, AND PROTECTIONIST POLICIES HAD ONLY MADE POOR COUNTRIES POORER. FREE-MARKET POLICIES, ON THE OTHER HAND, WOULD MAKE THEM EFFICIENT, COMPETITIVE, AND WORLD-CLASS.

SO THE IMF IMPOSED A KIND OF SHOCK THERAPY, SUPPOSEDLY TO RESTORE POOR ECONOMIES TO HEALTH AFTER THE "DISASTROUS" PATERNALISM IMPLEMENTED BY EARLIER REGIMES. THIS THERAPY INCLUDED SLASHING BUDGETS, CUTTING SOCIAL SERVICES, IMPLEMENTING AUSTERITY PROGRAMS, AND LAYING OFF HUGE NUMBERS OF PUBLIC SERVANTS.

TOGETHER WITH THE FOREIGN DEBT, THESE POLICIES CAUSED LIVING STANDARDS TO PLUMMET THROUGHOUT LATIN AMERICA.

THROUGH THE IMF LETTERS OF INTENTION, THE INTERNATIONAL FINANCIAL INSTITUTIONS PUSHED AN AGENDA BASED ON THREE BASIC POINTS.

1. FREE TRADE AND OPEN MARKETS.

2. REMOVE ALL LEGAL RESTRICTIONS ON THE WEALTHY.

3. SHRINK THE STATE AND PRIVATIZE STATE-OWNED ENTERPRISES, ASSETS, MINES, ETC.

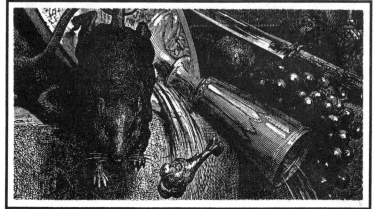

Drawings: Gustave Doré

WHAT THE NEOLIBERALS DIDN'T SAY IS THAT IN A WORLD ECONOMY DOMINATED BY MONOPOLIES, THE FREE MARKET ENABLES THESE HUGE CORPORATIONS TO SWALLOW UP ANYTHING THAT HAD BEEN PROTECTED, NAMELY SMALL NATIONAL ECONOMIES.

IN REALITY NEOLIBERALISM IS JUST A NEW TYPE OF IMPERIALISM.

NEOLIBERAL THEORY IS A PRODUCT PACKAGED FOR EXPORT TO UNDERDEVEL-OPED NATIONS. RICH COUNTRIES LIKE THE U.S., GERMANY, FRANCE, OR HOLLAND DON'T PRACTICE IT TO THE SAME DEGREE AT HOME BECAUSE THEIR CITIZENS WOULD BE UP IN ARMS AT THE CONSEQUENCES. YET NEOLIBERAL GURUS INSIST THAT IF POOR COUNTRIES FOLLOW THEIR ADVICE ABOUT FREE AND OPEN MAR-KETS, THEY'LL SOON BE MEMBERS OF THE FIRST WORLD CLUB.

ALL THAT TALK, HOWEVER, IS JUST A COVER. THE REAL PROGRAM IS TO MAKE SURE THE RICH COUNTRIES MAINTAIN CONTROL OF THE THIRD WORLD'S WEALTH AND RAW MATERIALS, AND HAVE ACCESS TO THEIR (CHEAP) LABOR.

THE CLAIM THAT NEOLIBERAL ORTHODOXY AS IMPOSED BY THE IMF LEADS TO GROWTH IS FAR FROM TRUE. AFTER ALL, THE "ASIAN TIGERS," SUCH AS SINGAPORE AND SOUTH KOREA, SUCCEEDED BECAUSE OF PROTECTIONIST POLICIES AND STRICT STATE CONTROLS—ON BUSINESSMEN AS WELL AS WORKERS. IN SOUTH KOREA, FOR INSTANCE, CAPITAL FLIGHT WAS A CAPITAL OFFENSE.

I say that if the poor countries are getting plundered it's because they don't have any entrepreneurial vision!

And since I have vision to spare, I'm going to turn my car wash into a business that can plunder and exploit with the best of them.

And I mean big-time. I'm going to plunder a really rich country.

Another drink, Charro?

Sure, why not?

Hey, your course is really working. Let's get on with it.

So where was I? The rich countries are rich because they take money from the poor.

13. HOW TO LEAVE THE THIRD WORLD BEHIND . . . AND FIND YOURSELF IN THE FOURTH

THE NEOLIBERAL AGENDA EXCLUDED LARGE SECTORS OF THE POPULATION FROM THE FORMAL ECONOMY. THE ABOLITION OF STATE PROGRAMS AND THE SALE OF STATE-OWNED COMPANIES LEFT MILLIONS DESTITUTE.

THE PROGRAMS CUT HAD PROVIDED A SOCIAL SAFETY NET TO HELP WITH FOOD, HOUSING, TRANSPORTATION, ETC. THE THREE-POINT NEOLIBERAL AGENDA SENT THE ECONOMY INTO A TAILSPIN AND SCREWED THE POOR.

FREE-TRADE AGREEMENTS AND OPEN MARKETS ARE ONLY GOOD FOR MULTINATIONAL CORPORATIONS. THEY UNDERCUT GOVERNMENT'S CAPACITY TO REGULATE INDUSTRY. WHAT'S MORE, THEY WEAKEN UNIONS, LEAVING WORKERS TO FEND FOR THEMSELVES.

LOCALLY OWNED FACTORIES IN COUNTRIES SUCH AS MEXICO WENT BELLY-UP AND WERE REPLACED BY NEW PLANTS, BUILT BY THE MULTINATIONALS. IN THESE *MAQUILADORAS*, WORKERS EARNED STARVATION WAGES IN HORRIBLE WORK-ING CONDITIONS. THAT'S HOW WAGES WERE DRIVEN DOWN ACROSS THE WORLD.

LOCAL BANKING WAS OPENED UP TO FOREIGN CAPITAL AND GRADUALLY TAKEN OVER BY THE BIG AMERICAN AND EUROPEAN LENDERS.

IN THIS WAY, ALL THE VITAL SECTORS OF THE THIRD WORLD'S ECONOMY PASSED INTO THE HANDS OF THE BIG MULTINATIONAL CORPORATIONS. WHEN RECESSION HITS THE U.S., THEY CLOSE THE *MAQUILADORAS* IN MEXICO AND THE PEOPLE WHO WORK THERE LOSE THEIR JOBS. IF A SPANISH OR U.S. BANK NEEDS A SHOT IN THE ARM, IT TAKES THE MONEY FROM MEXICO OR ANOTHER POOR COUNTRY.

THE OPENING OF THE GRAIN MARKET ACROSS THE WORLD FORCED MANY COMMUNITIES TO GIVE UP FARMING AND TO IMPORT THEIR FOOD. THIS IS DANGEROUS BECAUSE IF IMPORTS ARE CUT OFF, THERE COULD BE FAMINE, AS THERE WERE IN THE 19TH CENTURY. THIS DESTRUCTION OF LOCAL AGRICULTURE IS ONE OF NEOLIBERALISM'S WORST LEGACIES.

IN NEARLY ALL THIRD WORLD COUNTRIES, THE DEREGULATION OF CAPITAL—
REMOVING RESTRICTIONS ON INVESTMENT, OWNERSHIP, AND SPECULATION—
WAS ACHIEVED IN SHORT ORDER. NEW ELITES SPRANG UP AND MADE VAST FOR-
TUNES BY PLAYING FAST AND LOOSE WITH THE LAW.

IN MUCH OF THE WORLD, NEOLIBERAL PROGRAMS HAD THE EFFECT OF LEGALIZING
WHITE-COLLAR CRIME.

JUST AS THE 19TH-CENTURY INDUSTRIALISTS HAD SACKED AND DESTROYED LOCAL ECONOMIES, THE MODERN MULTINATIONALS ARE ALWAYS QUICK TO RUSH IN WHENEVER THERE'S A BUCK TO BE MADE. PARTICULARLY VULNERABLE ARE STATE-OWNED CORPORATIONS SUCH AS UTILITIES, OIL COMPANIES, ETC., WHICH ARE VITAL TO THE NATIONAL ECONOMY.

IN THE 19TH CENTURY, LOCAL ASSETS WERE SPREAD FAR AND WIDE; AT THE END OF THE 20TH CENTURY, HOWEVER, THEY WERE CONCENTRATED IN STATE-OWNED ENTERPRISES. AS A RESULT, WHEN THESE WERE PRIVATIZED, THE LARGE CONGLOMERATES WERE ABLE TO APPROPRIATE THE ASSETS OF ENTIRE NATIONS AT AMAZING SPEEDS.

WITH SUBSIDIES GONE, MILLIONS WENT HUNGRY.

BUT WHILE PREACHING THE END OF ALL STATE PATERNALISM, NEOLIBERAL GOVERNMENTS PROVIDED HUGE SUBSIDIES TO BIG BUSINESS AND THE WEALTHIEST ENTREPRENEURS.

We have to do away with big, costly and inefficient government...

So we can get on with our big, costly, and inefficient privatizations.

IN GENERAL THESE GOVERNMENTS ATTENDED TO THE NEEDS OF BUSINESS . . .
AND IGNORED THOSE OF THE MAJORITY.

THE NEOLIBERALS CARED LITTLE ABOUT THE SOCIAL COST OF THEIR POLICIES—
UNLIKE THE PEOPLE WHO HAD TO PAY IT.

14. GLOBALIZATION, A.K.A. ECONOMIC COLONIALISM

AS THE ECONOMIES OF POORER NATIONS DETERIORATED, SO DID THE
PROSPECTS OF STABILITY AND SECURITY. THIS LED TO CAPITAL FLIGHT TO
MORE SECURE HAVENS; ACCORDING TO *THE NEW YORK TIMES*, BETWEEN
$600 AND $800 BILLION LEFT LATIN AMERICA IN THE 1980s.

JUST AS IN THE 19TH CENTURY, FREE-MARKET POLICIES LED TO THE PLUNDER OF
POOR COUNTRIES.

THIS NEW FORM OF ECONOMIC COLONIALISM, WHICH BEGAN IN THE 1980s AND CONTINUES TO THIS DAY, IS COMMONLY KNOWN AS GLOBALIZATION, A FANCY TERM FOR THE SYSTEMATIC LOOTING OF THE THIRD WORLD BY WEALTHY NATIONS.

THE PILLAGING IS FAR WORSE THAN ANYTHING THE SPANISH CONQUISTADORS CAME UP WITH, AND WHO KNOWS WHEN IT WILL END?

THE FOREIGN DEBT IS ONE OF THE PRIMARY MEANS OF PLUNDER.

★ IN 1982, MEXICO BORROWED $57 BILLION FROM FOREIGN LENDERS.

★ BETWEEN 1982 AND 2002, MEXICO PAID $478 BILLION IN INTEREST ALONE, BORROWING MORE TO MAKE THE PAYMENTS.

★ BY THE YEAR 2002, MEXICO'S DEBT HAD INCREASED FROM $57 BILLION TO $157 BILLION, INCLUDING NEW DEBTS INCURRED TO PAY OFF EXISTING LOANS. PAYING THE DEBT TAKES THE LION'S SHARE OF THE BUDGET.

Right! He's come for the portion of the budget that goes to pay the foreign debt.

TELLER

IN OTHER WORDS, EVEN THOUGH MEXICO HAS PAID THE 1982 DEBT EIGHT TIMES OVER, IT STILL OWES THREE TIMES AS MUCH. BY 2010, THE PAYMENTS WILL BE STRATOSPHERIC.

IN SHORT, NEOLIBERAL GLOBALIZATION HELPS RICH COUNTRIES LOOK BETTER AND BETTER, WHILE THE POOR MIGHT AS WELL DROP OUT OF THE COMPETITION.

AS IN THE 19TH CENTURY, FREE-MARKET ECONOMICS ONLY ACCENTUATES THE DIFFERENCES.

THIRD WORLD MISERY FUELS FIRST WORLD WEALTH: DURING THE 1980S, IT WAS CASH TRANSFUSIONS FROM LATIN AMERICA THAT HELPED REACTIVATE THE U.S. ECONOMY.

Yes, I know the price of milk went up, dear, but look how cheap caviar is and Châteauneuf du Pape . . .

THE STAMPEDE TOWARD GLOBALIZATION DROVE GOVERNMENTS THAT ONCE PROMOTED THE WELFARE STATE TO LINE UP BEHIND WASHINGTON AND EMBRACE NEOLIBERAL POLICIES. THIS HAPPENED WITH FRANÇOIS MITTERRAND IN FRANCE, FELIPE GONZÁLEZ IN SPAIN, THE P. R. I. IN MEXICO . . .

Hello, we're the neosocial democratic government.

15. THE FALL OF THE SOCIALIST BLOC

THE NEOLIBER-AL GOVERN-MENTS OF THATCHER, REAGAN, AND THEN BUSH WERE ON A ROLL. THEY SET THEIR SIGHTS ON THE SOCIALIST BLOC.

Frankly I don't get why the capitalist countries are so bent on discrediting and destroying the socialist countries . . .

. . . since they're doing such a good job of it on their own.

BY THE MIDDLE OF THE 1980s, NONE OF THE SUPPOSEDLY SOCIALIST SYSTEMS WERE SUSTAINABLE. IN COUNTRIES SUCH AS NORTH KOREA AND CHINA, THE GOVERNMENTS WERE ALSO REPRESSIVE AND TOTALITARIAN.

IN 1989, AT TIANANMEN SQUARE IN BEIJING, THE REGIME OF DENG XIAO PING VIOLENTLY REPRESSED A STUDENT UPRISING.

UNDER MIKHAIL GORBACHEV, THE SOVIET COMMUNIST PARTY TRIED TO UNDERTAKE DEMOCRATIC REFORMS, BUT IT WAS TOO LATE: PEOPLE WERE FED UP WITH YEARS OF OPPRESSION AND BUREAUCRATIC INEFFICIENCY. FINALLY, IN 1991, THE LONG EXPERIMENT IN SOVIET SOCIALISM CAME TO AN END, VICTIM OF ITS INTERNAL CONTRADICTIONS AS WELL AS OF THE POLICIES OF THATCHER AND BUSH. THE COLLAPSE WAS WITHOUT A DOUBT A VICTORY FOR THE PEOPLE.

HOWEVER, IT WAS ALSO A VICTORY FOR THE FREE-MARKET CHAMPIONS, WHO SAW IN THE FORMER SOCIALIST COUNTRIES NEW MARKETS, NEW SUPPLIES OF CHEAP LABOR AND RAW MATERIALS, TECHNOLOGIES TO STEAL, ETC.

BECAUSE THE STALINISTS HAD KILLED OFF ANY OPPOSITION FROM THE LEFT, WHEN THE PEOPLE FINALLY ROSE UP AGAINST THE STALINIST BUREAUCRACY, IT WAS UNDER THE BANNER OF CAPITALISM—WHICH, GIVEN THE CIRCUMSTANCES, WAS AS REVOLUTIONARY AS THINGS COULD GET.

THE ONLY SOCIALIST ENCLAVES LEFT WERE CUBA, NORTH KOREA, AND CHINA (WHICH WAS ALREADY EXPERIMENTING WITH THE MARKET ECONOMY). THE COLLAPSE OF SOCIALISM AS A VIABLE POLITICAL ALTERNATIVE CAME AS A BLOW TO WORKING-CLASS MOVEMENTS AND OPPRESSED PEOPLES WORLDWIDE.

WHAT COLLAPSED, OF COURSE, WAS THE MORIBUND PARTY BUREAU-CRACY—A LEGACY OF STALIN. THE BUREAUCRATS, KNOWN AS THE *NOMENKLATURA*, WERE SELF-SERVING, UNPRINCIPLED OPPOR-TUNISTS. AND THE MAN WHO LED THE CAMPAIGN TO TRANSFORM THE USSR INTO A MARKET ECONO-MY WAS BORIS YELTSIN, WHO NOT LONG BEFORE HAD BEEN AN OLD STALINIST BUREAUCRAT ...

THE SOCIALIST BLOC WAS A DISASTER IN MANY RESPECTS, BUT FOR THE THIRD WORLD, AT LEAST, IT HAD SERVED TO CHECK THE RAPACITY OF THE MONOPOLIES. ONCE IT WAS OUT OF THE WAY, CAPITALISM WAS FREE TO UNLEASH ITS FULL BRUTE FORCE ...

Sorry, but I don't see the Third World delegates raising a glass to the New World Order.

You don't? They're the ones serving the drinks.

CCI

USA

16. NEW WORLD ORDER OR NEW WORLD CHAOS?

THE FALL OF SOCIALISM, COMBINED WITH THE COLLAPSE OF THE WELFARE STATE, WAS A GREAT TRIUMPH FOR THE BUSINESS ELITE. WITH THE CLOSE OF THE COLD WAR IN THE EARLY 1990s, A NEW WORLD ORDER EMERGED IN WHICH THE USA—THE HOME OF THE BIGGEST BUSINESSES—WAS THE SOLE SUPERPOWER AND THE WORLD'S POLICEMAN.

NOT SINCE THE COLONIAL EMPIRES OF THE 19TH CENTURY HAD THE FREE MARKET REIGNED SUPREME OVER THE ENTIRE WORLD.

LED BY WASHINGTON AND ARMED WITH UNPRECEDENTED ECONOMIC, TECH-
NOLOGICAL, AND MILITARY MIGHT, THE CAPITALIST COUNTRIES CHARGED
HEADLONG INTO A NEW ERA OF WORLD COLONIZATION.

WASHINGTON WORKED CLOSELY WITH THE OLD COLONIAL POWERS SUCH AS GREAT BRITAIN, FRANCE, JAPAN, AND BELGIUM, AND WITH INTERNATIONAL INSTITUTIONS SUCH AS THE IMF AND THE WORLD TRADE ORGANIZATION. TOGETHER THEY CONCOCTED ECONOMIC POLICIES FOR THE THIRD WORLD, WHILE POOR PEOPLE WERE PUT OUT TO PASTURE...

FROM THE 1980s ON, THIRD WORLD NATIONS HAD NO SAY IN RUNNING THEIR OWN ECONOMIES. INSTEAD OF BEING GOVERNED BY LEADERS WHO CARED FOR THE WELFARE OF THE PEOPLE, THEY WERE ADMINISTERED BY MANAGERS HIRED BY BIG BUSINESS, WHO RAN THE COUNTRIES AS IF THEY WERE CORPORATE ENTERPRISES.

THIS WAS THE CASE WITH ZEDILLO IN MEXICO, CARDOSO IN BRAZIL, AND MENEM IN ARGENTINA, AMONG OTHERS. TO TOP IT OFF, IN 2000, A FORMER EXECUTIVE OF COCA-COLA, VICENTE FOX, BECAME PRESIDENT OF MEXICO.

WITH SOCIALIST AND COMMUNIST PARTIES OUT OF THE PICTURE, AND SOCIAL-DEMOCRATIC GROUPS UNDERCUTTING THEIR OWN LEGITIMACY BY EMBRACING NEOLIBERAL ECONOMICS, THE COAST WAS CLEAR FOR CONSERVATIVE PARTIES TO STEP IN, SUCH AS HAPPENED IN SPAIN WITH AZNAR AND MEXICO WITH FOX.

THAT'S THE STORY OF FREE-TRADE DEMOCRACIES.

WASHINGTON CLAIMS THAT THIS IS THE ULTIMATE TRIUMPH OF DEMOCRATIC GOVERNMENT. BUT NEVER BEFORE HAVE SO MANY PEOPLE BEEN SO IGNORED OR SO GROUND DOWN BY ECONOMIC SHOCK THERAPIES AND AUSTERITY PLANS.

DEMOCRATIC FACADES HELP KEEP THE BUSINESS OLIGARCHS IN POWER, ALLOWING THEM TO IMPOSE THEIR DEADLY EFFICIENT PROGRAMS ALL ACROSS THE WORLD.

DESPITE THE WIDESPREAD BELIEF THAT UNDER THE FREE MARKET THE PRESS IS FREER THAN EVER, THE FACT IS THAT THE MASS MEDIA OBEY THE DICTATES OF THEIR OWNERS—WHO ARE, OF COURSE, BIG BUSINESSMEN. TELEVISION AND NEWSPAPERS PROMOTE THE INTERESTS OF THEIR ADVERTISERS, AND FOR NEWS, THEY RELY ON INFORMATION SUPPLIED BY THE POWERFUL.

BIG BUSINESS CONTROLS THE MEDIA AS NEVER BEFORE, AND CHOOSES WHICH ISSUES GET DEBATED ... AND WHICH DO NOT.

AS WE'VE SEEN, THE LOGIC OF CAPITALISM WAS ALWAYS AT ODDS WITH BASIC ETHICAL PRINCIPLES. BUT NEOLIBERAL CAPITALISM HAS ABANDONED ETHICS ALTOGETHER. ITS EFFECTS ARE NASTY ENOUGH IN THE RICH COUNTRIES, BUT FAR WORSE IN THE DEVELOPING WORLD.

IT HAS EXCLUDED WHOLE COUNTRIES, LIKE BOLIVIA AND PARAGUAY, AND ENTIRE CONTINENTS, LIKE AFRICA, CONSIGNING THEIR INHABITANTS TO CONTINUED POVERTY. IT HAS EVEN DESTROYED A NUMBER OF PROSPEROUS ECONOMIES, SUCH AS ARGENTINA'S.

WHAT'S MORE, UNDER THESE CONDITIONS, PEOPLE CAN'T DO MUCH TO DEFEND THEMSELVES; THE OPPOSITION HAS BEEN SO BEATEN DOWN, IT HAS NO ALTERNATIVES TO OFFER. EVEN UNIONS HAVE BEGUN TO TALK LIKE BUSINESS-MEN.

ACCORDING TO ITS OWN PREDICTIONS, THE U.S. SHOULDN'T HAVE HAD TO WAGE ANY MORE WARS AFTER THE FALL OF THE SOCIALIST BLOC, BUT THAT'S NOT HOW IT'S TURNED OUT. THE RULE OF BUSINESS IS VIOLENT AND REPRESSIVE BY NATURE.

EVER SINCE GLOBALIZATION BEGAN, WASHINGTON HAS NEVER STOPPED WAGING WAR: FROM THE INVASION OF PANAMA TO SUPPORT FOR THE NICARAGUAN CONTRAS TO THE WAR ON DRUGS, WHICH IT INVOKES TO JUSTIFY CONTINUED INTERVENTION IN LATIN AMERICA.

AND IN THE MIDDLE EAST, WASHINGTON HAS GONE ON SUPPORTING ISRAEL WITH MONEY AND WEAPONS IN ITS ONGOING AGGRESSION AGAINST THE PALESTINIANS, KEEPING THE REGION IN A PERMANENT STATE OF CONFLICT.

Cartoon: Helguera

SOON, WASHINGTON WAS ALSO SUPPORTING A VARIETY OF FUNDAMENTALIST ISLAMIC GROUPS, THANKS TO EVENTS IN THE CENTRAL ASIAN COUNTRY OF AFGHANISTAN.

IN THE LATE 1970s, THE USSR INVADED AFGHANISTAN TO KEEP A FRIENDLY GOVERNMENT IN POWER. THE UNITED STATES HELPED ARM AND TRAIN ISLAMIC MILITANTS, KNOWN AS THE MUJAHEDIN, TO COMBAT THE SOVIETS. AFTER THE SOVIETS FINALLY WITHDREW IN 1989, BRUTAL FIGHTING AMONG MUJAHEDIN FACTIONS BROUGHT TO POWER A GROUP OF ULTRA-CONSERVATIVE RELIGIOUS FANATICS KNOWN AS THE TALIBAN. THEY IMPOSED A NUMBER OF HARSH LAWS AND MEDIEVAL HORRORS, ESPECIALLY ON WOMEN.

AMONG THE MUJAHEDIN SUPPORTED AND TRAINED BY THE CIA, THERE WAS A YOUNG MILLIONAIRE OF SAUDI ORIGIN, WHO WOULD LATER GARNER A LOT OF ATTENTION: OSAMA BIN LADEN.

WASHINGTON'S GOAL IN ALL THIS WAS CONTROL OF THE MIDDLE EAST, HOME TO THE WORLD'S LARGEST OIL RESERVES. OIL WAS BEHIND THE CONSTANT POSTURING AGAINST IRAN, AS WELL AS THE IRAN-IRAQ WAR OF 1980—88, WHERE THE U.S. SUPPORTED THE IRAQI DICTATOR SADDAM HUSSEIN AGAINST THE IRANIAN SHIITES. OF COURSE, OIL WAS ALSO BEHIND THE WAR FOUGHT AGAINST THE SAME SADDAM HUSSEIN IN 1991 AND 2003.

OF COURSE, THERE WAS NO DEFENSE FOR A DICTATORSHIP LIKE HUSSEIN'S, BUT THAT DIDN'T STOP WASHINGTON FROM DEFENDING THE MAN FOR YEARS, OR THE MULTINATIONALS FROM DOING BUSINESS WITH HIM.

17. GLOBAPHOBES OF THE WORLD, UNITE!

A HUGE AMOUNT OF MONEY WENT STRAIGHT FROM THE POOR COUNTRIES TO THE UNITED STATES, BUT MOST OF ITS CITIZENS NEVER SAW ANY OF IT. THE U.S. HAS THE HIGHEST POVERTY RATE OF ALL INDUSTRIALIZED NATIONS. ACCORDING TO ITS OWN CENSUS BUREAU, IN 2001:

★ 32.9 MILLION U.S. CITIZENS LIVED IN POVERTY—THAT'S 11.7%.

★ 13.4 MILLION LIVED IN EXTREME POVERTY.

★ 1.3 MILLION FELL BELOW THE POVERTY LINE BETWEEN 2000 AND 2001.

★ 800,000 FELL INTO EXTREME POVERTY IN THE SAME PERIOD.

★ 22.7% OF AFRICAN-AMERICANS AND 22.4% OF HISPANIC AMERICANS ARE OFFICIALLY POOR.

DURING THE 1990s, THE U.S. ECONOMY ROSE TO UNPRECEDENTED HEIGHTS, BUT SO DID SOCIAL INEQUALITY. IN 2001, ONE-FIFTH OF THE NATION OWNED ONE-HALF OF THE NATIONAL WEALTH, WHILE THE POOREST 20 PERCENT OWNED ONLY 3.5 PERCENT. BUT ON THE GLOBAL LEVEL, THE DISPROPORTION IS FAR WORSE.

THE GAP BETWEEN THE FIRST AND THIRD WORLDS WIDENED DRAMATICALLY WITHIN A FEW SHORT YEARS, SO THAT AT THE DAWN OF THE 21ST CENTURY, 80 PERCENT OF THE WORLD'S POPULATION WERE LIVING WITHOUT BASIC ESSENTIALS. BUT THE NEOLIBERALS COULDN'T CARE LESS ABOUT THE SOCIAL COST OF MODERNIZATION.

IN AFRICA, THIS SOCIAL COST WAS HORRENDOUS. TWO DECADES OF FREE-MARKET RESTRUCTURING RUINED MUCH OF THE CONTINENT'S PRODUCTIVE CAPACITY AND LEFT MOST OF IT COMPLETELY IMPOVERISHED.

★ IN 1990, 242 MILLION PEOPLE IN SUB-SAHARAN AFRICA LIVED ON LESS THAN A DOLLAR A DAY.

★ IN 2002, 302 MILLION PEOPLE THERE LIVED ON LESS THAN A DOLLAR A DAY.

★ ACCORDING TO THE MOST RECENT FIGURES, 78% LIVE ON LESS THAN TWO DOLLARS A DAY.

AFRICA'S INFANT MORTALITY RATE IS 60 PERCENT HIGHER THAN THE AVER-AGE FOR ALL DEVELOPING COUNTRIES. LIFE EXPECTANCY IS ABOUT FORTY-SEVEN YEARS, PRIMARILY DUE TO AIDS, WHICH KILLS 2.3 MILLION PEOPLE EACH YEAR. IN BOTSWANA, 36 PERCENT OF ALL ADULTS ARE INFECTED WITH HIV; 25 PERCENT IN SWAZILAND AND ZIMBABWE; 20 PERCENT IN SOUTH AFRICA.

THE SITUATION IN LATIN AMERICA IS ALSO SERIOUS. AS FREE TRADE EXPAND-
ED, THE NUMBER OF POOR PEOPLE CLIMBED STEADILY IN EVERY COUNTRY OF
THE REGION. ACCORDING TO THE WORLD BANK:

★ IN 1986, 137.5 MILLION PEOPLE (33.7% OF THE POPULATION) LIVED ON LESS
   THAN TWO DOLLARS A DAY, AND 54.2 MILLION (13.3%) LIVED ON LESS THAN
   ONE DOLLAR A DAY.

★ BY 1998, THERE WERE 179.8 MILLION PEOPLE (35.8% OF THE POPULATION)
   SOMEHOW GETTING BY ON LESS THAN TWO DOLLARS A DAY, AND 78 MILLION
   (15.5%) PERFORMING THE DAILY MIRACLE OF LIVING ON LESS THAN A DOLLAR.

THE FIGURES FROM OTHER SOURCES ARE EVEN MORE ALARMING.

ACCORDING TO THE INTER-AMERICAN DEVELOPMENT BANK (IDB), THE DISTRIBUTION OF WEALTH IN LATIN AMERICA IS VERY UNEVEN: THE RICHEST 10 PERCENT EARN 84 TIMES MORE THAN THE POOREST 19 PERCENT.

CHILDREN ARE PARTICULARLY HARD HIT. IDB FIGURES FOR THE REGION IN 2001 SHOW:

★ 58% OF CHILDREN LIVE IN EXTREME POVERTY.
★ ONE OF THREE CHILDREN UNDER THE AGE OF TWO IS MALNOURISHED.
★ SINGLE MOTHERS HEAD 30% OF ALL HOUSEHOLDS.
★ THE NUMBER OF HOMELESS CHILDREN IS GROWING AT AN DISTURBING RATE, AND IT IS UNKNOWN HOW MANY OF THESE ARE SURVIVING ON THEIR OWN.

IN 1940, ARGENTINA WAS ONE OF THE TOP TEN ECONOMIC POWERS IN THE WORLD, WITH A LIVING STANDARD HIGHER THAN THE LATIN AMERICAN AVERAGE, A LARGE MIDDLE CLASS, AND A PREDOMINANTLY URBAN POPULATION OF 90 PERCENT.

SINCE THE 1980S, THE COUNTRY HAS FOLLOWED THE IMF DICTATES TO THE LETTER, PRIVATIZING AND OPENING ITS MARKETS TO FREE TRADE.

AND SURE ENOUGH, IN 1994, ARGENTINA WENT INTO A RAPID DECLINE.

★ IN 1994, 21.6% OF THE URBAN POPULATION LIVED IN POVERTY; 3.7% IN EXTREME POVERTY.

★ IN 1998, 29.4% OF THE URBAN POPULATION LIVED IN POVERTY; 7.1% IN EXTREME POVERTY.

BETWEEN 1960 AND 1980 THE NUMBER OF POOR PEOPLE IN MEXICO HOVERED STEADILY AROUND 30 MILLION. BY 1998, ACCORDING TO THE WORLD BANK, 43.4 MILLION (43 PERCENT OF THE POPULATION) LIVED ON LESS THAN TWO DOLLARS A DAY, WHILE 18.2 MILLION LIVED ON LESS THAN ONE.

ON TOP OF THAT, BEFORE THE NEW POLICIES WERE PUT INTO EFFECT, BASIC GOODS WERE SUBSIDIZED BY THE GOVERNMENT, SO A DOLLAR WENT A LOT FURTHER IN 1980 THAN IT DID IN 1998. OTHER SOURCES, ONCE AGAIN, PAINT A MUCH BLEAKER PICTURE.

ACCORDING TO THE MEXICAN GOVERNMENT ITSELF, IN 2002:

★ 53.7% OF MEXICAN CITIZENS (59 MILLION) LIVED IN POVERTY.

★ 24.2 MILLION COULD NOT COVER THEIR BASIC NUTRITIONAL NEEDS.

AND FROM A MORE RELIABLE SOURCE, THE COLEGIO DE MÉXICO:

★ 76.8% OF MEXICANS (84.5 MILLION) WERE LIVING IN POVERTY IN 2002.

WHILE THIRTY-SEVEN BIG BUSINESSMEN CONTROL NEARLY A QUARTER OF EVERYTHING MEXICO PRODUCES, 70 PERCENT OF THE POPULATION HAVE TO DIVVY UP A THIRD OF THE NATION'S WEALTH.

ACCORDING TO THE MEXICAN GOVERNMENT:

★ 43% OF CHILDREN UNDER FIVE LIVE IN POVERTY OR EXTREME POVERTY.

★ 30% UNDER FIVE WHO LIVE IN POVERTY SUFFER FROM MALNUTRITION.

★ NEARLY ALL RURAL HOUSEHOLDS LIVE IN POVERTY OR EXTREME POVERTY.

★ 14% OF MEXICAN HOUSEHOLDS HAVE NO RUNNING WATER.

★ 9 OUT OF 10 INDIGENOUS HOUSEHOLDS LIVE IN EXTREME POVERTY.

NEOLIBERALISM IS AN UNDECLARED WAR AGAINST ENTIRE SECTORS OF THE POPULATION. IN MEXICO, THE INDIGENOUS PEOPLES SUFFER THE MOST.

IT'S HARD TO SAY WHETHER THE MEXICAN ECONOMY IS HEADED FOR A CRISIS LIKE ARGENTINA'S, BUT IT'S VERY CLEAR THAT THE PEOPLE HAVE SUFFERED GREATLY. CONSEQUENTLY, THEY HAVE ACTIVELY FOUGHT THE NEOLIBERAL AGENDA AT EVERY STEP: FROM THE DISPUTED ELECTIONS OF 1988, TO THE HUGE "EL BARZON" MOVEMENT OF SMALL DEBTORS RESISTING FORECLOSURES, TO THE ZAPATISTA INSURRECTION OF 1994.

DESPITE WIDESPREAD MOBILIZATION, HOWEVER, LOCAL ACTIONS ARE NO MATCH FOR A GLOBAL FORCE. THE CAPITALISTS ARE STRONGER THAN EVER AND THE PEOPLE ARE DIVIDED, LACKING BOTH POLITICAL LEADERSHIP AND VIABLE GLOBAL ALTERNATIVES.

NEVERTHELESS, THE CHIAPAS REVOLT OF NEW YEAR'S EVE 1993 WAS A GOOD REMINDER THAT IF WAR IS DECLARED ON THE WRETCHED OF THE EARTH, THEY JUST MIGHT FIGHT BACK, AS THEY HAVE IN THE PAST.

IN MEXICO, THE MAYAN GROUPS, ORGANIZED IN THE ZAPATISTA NATIONAL LIBERATION ARMY, UNDERSTOOD CLEARLY THAT THEIR MISERY WAS THE RESULT OF A GLOBAL PROJECT.

THE ZAPATISTA REBELLION REMINDED THE WORLD THAT THE APPARENT ECO-NOMIC BOOM IS REALLY BUILT ON A GLOBAL BUST THAT HAS IMPOVERISHED MILLIONS—AND THAT THE IMPOVERISHED ARE PREPARED TO FIGHT FOR THEIR RIGHTS.

IT MADE THE WORLD TAKE NOTICE OF THE DARK SIDE OF NEOLIBERALISM.

APART FROM HAVING A CLEVER RHETORICAL STYLE, THE ZAPATISTAS ALSO PROMOTED A HUMANIST ALTERNATIVE TO THE POLICIES PROPOSED BY BIG BUSINESS.

BY ROUSING THE CONSCIENCE OF PEOPLE AROUND THE WORLD, THEY LAUNCHED A NEW GLOBAL STRUGGLE AGAINST GLOBALIZATION.

LITTLE BY LITTLE, THE RESISTANCE GREW. IN 1999, ACTIVISTS GATHERED IN SEATTLE TO PROTEST AT THE MEETING OF THE WORLD TRADE ORGANIZATION.

A LARGE NUMBER OF THE PROTESTORS WERE U.S. CITIZENS. THEIR ACTIVE STANCE AGAINST THE CORPORATIONS OF THEIR OWN COUNTRY SHOWED REMARKABLE SOLIDARITY WITH THE WORLD'S POOR. SUCH SOLIDARITY HAD NOT BEEN SEEN SINCE THE PROTESTS AGAINST THE VIETNAM WAR.

WHEREVER CAPITALISM'S HEAD HONCHOS GATHER, THEY ARE MET WITH PROTESTS. IN GENOA IN 2001, THERE WERE MASSIVE DEMONSTRATIONS AT THE MEETING OF THE G8, THE LEADERS OF THE EIGHT RICHEST INDUSTRIAL NATIONS. MOST OF THE PROTESTS WERE PEACEFUL. BUT RADICAL GROUPS PROVOKED A SERIOUS CONFRONTATION WITH THE SECURITY FORCES AND ONE DEMONSTRATOR WAS KILLED.

MASS RESISTANCE TO GLOBALIZATION COINCIDED WITH A SERIES OF CRISES FOR THE GLOBALIZERS.

18. A MUDDLED MODEL

WITH LITTLE TO OPPOSE IT, THE FREE MARKET SWALLOWED THE ENTIRE GLOB-
AL ECONOMY . . . AND YET, THERE IS CRISIS AFTER CRISIS.

BECAUSE EVERYTHING IS GLOBALLY CONNECTED, A CRISIS IN ONE CORNER OF
THE WORLD CAN SEND SHOCKWAVES ACROSS THE PLANET. SPECULATION IN
INDONESIA COULD—AND DID—RUIN SOUTH AMERICA.

SINCE THE SYSTEM IS DESIGNED TO SERVE THE BIG MONEY INTERESTS, IF A BANK NEEDS A SUDDEN CASH INFUSION, IT SIMPLY LIQUIDATES A FACTORY OR FARM SOMEWHERE IN THE WORLD, WHICH MIGHT HELP THE LIQUIDATORS BUT NOT THE LIQUIDATED.

IN THIS WAY THE FREE MARKET CAN ACTUALLY UNDERCUT PRODUCTION, WHICH IS THE SOURCE OF ALL WEALTH, EVEN FOR THE SPECULATORS. WHAT THE MODEL SUCCEEDS IN PRODUCING MORE OF EVERY YEAR IS CRISIS, POVERTY, AND MISERY.

THE MORE COMPANIES THAT GET LIQUIDATED, THE MORE PRODUCTIVE CAPACITY SHRINKS. AS LAYOFFS INCREASE, CONSUMPTION DROPS. SOONER OR LATER THE WHOLE ECONOMY GRINDS TO A HALT, WHICH IS KNOWN AS A RECESSION.

WHEN RECESSION HITS ECONOMICALLY POWERFUL NATIONS—AS HAPPENED IN THE U.S. IN 2001—LOOK OUT!

THE FIRST PLACES TO GET SHUT DOWN ARE THE ONES THAT ARE THE EASIEST FOR THE MULTINATIONALS TO CLOSE—NAMELY, THE *MAQUILADORAS*. FOR COUNTRIES LIKE MEXICO, WHERE THE OLD LOCALLY-OWNED FACTORIES HAD BEEN SACRIFICED ON THE ALTAR OF NEOLIBERALISM, THIS WAS A DISASTER.

IN 2001, MEXICO LOST A QUARTER OF A MILLION JOBS IN JUST SIX MONTHS, AND THE GOVERNMENT COULDN'T DO A THING TO HELP THE WORKERS.

ANOTHER FLAW IN THE MODEL IS THE RAMPANT CORRUPTION IN THE HIGH ECHELONS OF THE MULTINATIONALS. AT THE END OF 2001, A SCANDAL BROKE AT ENRON, AN ENERGY COMPANY WHOSE EXECUTIVES HAD COOKED THE BOOKS TO DEFRAUD THE PUBLIC AND LINE THEIR OWN POCKETS—AT A COST OF $30 BILLION DOLLARS TO THE STOCKHOLDERS. SIMILAR SCANDALS FOLLOWED AT WORLDCOM AND OTHER LARGE CORPORATIONS. MANY OF THESE COMPANIES HAD CLOSE TIES WITH THE BUSH ADMINISTRATION.

THE SCANDALS CAUSED CONSUMER CONFIDENCE IN THE FINANCIAL MARKETS TO PLUMMET, AND BETWEEN JANUARY AND SEPTEMBER OF 2002, THE U.S. STOCK EXCHANGES LOST A TOTAL OF $400 BILLION.

WORST OF ALL, WHEN THE U.S. CRISIS SPREAD, THE IMF RESPONDED BY FORCING THIRD WORLD COUNTRIES TO CUT BACK ON SOCIAL SPENDING, WHICH DEEPENED THE RECESSION AND FAILED TO REVIVE THE ECONOMY.

BY THE MIDDLE OF 2001, EVEN ALAN GREENSPAN, CHAIRMAN OF THE FEDERAL RESERVE BOARD, WAS ADMITTING THAT THE RECESSION FACING THE U.S. WOULD BE LONG AND DIFFICULT. THE COUNTRY WAS OBVIOUSLY IN A TIGHT SPOT, BUT WHAT HAPPENED ON SEPTEMBER 11, 2001 CAUSED A COMPLETE BREAKDOWN.

19. SEPTEMBER 11, 2001

ON THE MORNING OF SEPTEMBER 11, 2001, SUICIDE COMMANDOS FLEW HIJACKED PASSENGER PLANES INTO THE WORLD TRADE CENTER IN NEW YORK AND INTO THE PENTAGON IN WASHINGTON, DC.

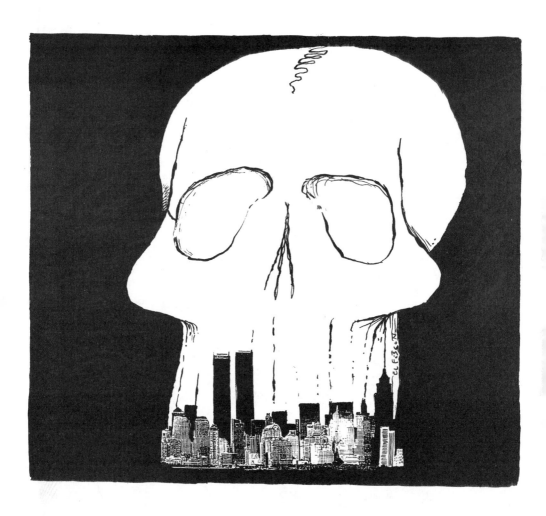

THE TWIN TOWERS COLLAPSED, KILLING THOUSANDS OF INNOCENT VICTIMS AND SOWING TERROR THROUGHOUT THE U.S. AND THE WORLD. NEARLY THREE THOUSAND PEOPLE DIED, MAKING THIS THE SINGLE WORST TERRORIST ACT IN HISTORY.

IT WAS ALSO THE FIRST TIME SINCE PEARL HARBOR THAT AN ATTACK LIKE THIS WAS CARRIED OUT ON U.S. TERRITORY—AND THE ONLY TIME THAT U.S. CIVILIANS WERE THE VICTIMS.

THE TARGETS WERE SYMBOLS OF U.S. ECONOMIC AND MILITARY POWER. AS A RESULT OF THE ATTACK, WORLD FINANCIAL MARKETS WENT INTO A PANIC, SEVERELY DEEPENING A RECESSION THAT WAS ALREADY IN PROGRESS.

WHILE THERE WERE SOME WHO CLAIMED THE MURDERS WERE A JUSTIFIED ACT OF POLITICAL VIOLENCE, NOTHING WHATSOEVER CAN JUSTIFY SUCH A HORRIFIC CRIME.

HORROR DOES NOT JUSTIFY...   HORROR DOES NOT JUSTIFY...   HORROR DOES NOT...   JUSTIFY HORROR...

BY THE SAME TOKEN, NOTHING CAN JUSTIFY USING THIS ATTACK AS A PRETEXT FOR LAUNCHING EQUALLY HORRIFIC ATTACKS BY THE UNITED STATES.

WHAT MADE THE ATTACKS PARTICULARLY TERRIFYING WAS THAT NO GROUP CLAIMED RESPONSIBILITY. THIS GAVE RISE TO ALL SORTS OF THEORIES.

WEEKS AFTER THE ATTACK, THE ONLY THING EVERYONE KNEW FOR SURE WAS THAT IT WAS AN UTTERLY CONTEMPTIBLE ACT OF TERROR.

A "TERRORIST" IS A PERSON OR GROUP THAT CARRIES OUT VIOLENT ACTS AS A MEANS TO OBTAIN POLITICAL ENDS.

The most savage terrorist acts are those in which innocent people are killed.

TERRORISM IS USUALLY A LAST RECOURSE FOR GROUPS THAT DO NOT BELIEVE PEACEFUL CHANGE IS POSSIBLE—BUT, OF COURSE, TERRORISM ITSELF IS HARDLY A VIABLE OPTION EITHER.

Terrorism is a serious problem.

It's violent, cruel, and inhuman.

And it only begets more terror.

TERRORISM IS UNACCEPTABLE AS A FORM OF STRUGGLE. YET IT IS COMMON IN MANY PARTS OF THE WORLD AND IS PROBABLY FUELED BY THE SOCIAL INEQUITY, POLITICAL EXCLUSION, AND OVERALL VIOLENCE OF THE NEOLIBERAL SYSTEM.

A WORLD OF SOCIAL INJUSTICE IS A WORLD WHERE TERRORISM CAN THRIVE.

NB: Rural guerrilla warfare is something entirely different.

20. THE MESS IN WASHINGTON

TO SEE HOW TERRORISM LEADS TO HARD-LINE REACTIONS, JUST LOOK AT THE SPEECH GEORGE BUSH MADE RIGHT AFTER THE ATTACKS. HE VOWED TO TAKE REVENGE AND DECLARED WAR ON ALL TERRORISM EVERYWHERE (EXCEPT, OF COURSE, THAT WHICH IS PERPETRATED BY THE U.S. OR ITS ALLIES).

THE ATTACKS BROUGHT ABOUT A MAJOR SHIFT IN WASHINGTON'S FOREIGN POLICY, AND SINCE WASHINGTON IS THE HUB OF OUR GLOBALIZED ECONOMY, THAT MEANT A SHIFT IN POLICY WORLDWIDE.

IN HIS SPEECH, BUSH DEMANDED THAT THE REST OF THE WORLD JOIN HIS ANTITERRORIST CRUSADE. EITHER YOU ARE WITH US, HE SAID, OR YOU ARE WITH THE TERRORISTS ... AND WILL BE TREATED AS SUCH, WITH THE FULL FORCE OF THE U.S. MILITARY.

THE PRESIDENT BLAMED THE ATTACK ON THE MUSLIM FUNDAMENTALIST GROUP AL QAEDA, LED BY OSAMA BIN LADEN, AND DEMANDED THAT THE TALIBAN GOVERNMENT IN AFGHANISTAN HAND OVER BIN LADEN OR FACE AN INVASION.

THIS WAS A
NEW KIND OF
WAR, BUSH
PROCLAIMED,
ONE THAT
WOULD NOT
END SOON—
CERTAINLY NOT
WHILE HE WAS
IN POWER.
AND AFTER
AFGHANISTAN
IT MIGHT NEED
TO BE FOUGHT
IN OTHER
COUNTRIES.

IN SPEAKING OUT AGAINST THE FUNDAMENTALIST TALIBAN REGIME, BUSH HIM-
SELF USED SIMILARLY FUNDAMENTALIST RHETORIC, INVOKING GOD AND CALLING
FOR THE DESTRUCTION OF THE "EVILDOERS" AND THE "EVIL ONES."

AND, FINALLY,
BUSH DECLARED
THAT THIS WAR
DEMANDED
GREATER SECRE-
CY AND THERE-
FORE THE PUBLIC
WOULD ONLY BE
KEPT PARTIALLY
INFORMED.

BUSH'S REACTION WAS MENACING, DANGEROUS, AND FULL OF CONTRADIC-
TIONS, RAISING MANY DOUBTS AND QUESTIONS, SUCH AS:

1. ISN'T RESPONDING TO TERRORISM WITH FULL-SCALE WAR TANTAMOUNT TO EMBRACING THE LOGIC OF TERRORISM AND ESCALATING THE CYCLE OF VIO-LENCE?

2. THE TALIBAN WERE HORRIBLE, BUT WHAT RIGHT DID THAT GIVE THE U.S. TO INVADE ANOTHER COUNTRY AND OVERTHROW ITS GOVERNMENT?

3. IF WE ACCEPT THE IDEA THAT THE U.S. MAY INVADE OTHER COUNTRIES IN ORDER TO COMBAT TERRORISM, ISN'T THAT THE SAME AS SAYING THAT U.S. INTERESTS OUTWEIGH THE SOVEREIGNTY OF OTHER NATIONS?

4. USUALLY PEOPLE WANT WARS TO BE OVER WITH AS QUICKLY AS POSSIBLE. SO WHY DOES BUSH WANT THIS ONE TO GO ON FOR YEARS, AND WHY DOES HE WANT TO EXPAND IT TO OTHER COUNTRIES?

5. THE STRUGGLE AGAINST TERRORISM IS A STRUGGLE AGAINST CRUELTY AND VIOLENCE. BUT DOESN'T WAR INFLICT CRUELTY AND VIOLENCE ON MILLIONS OF INNOCENT PEOPLE?

6. BUSH DEMANDED UNCONDITIONAL INTERNATIONAL SUPPORT FOR ATTACKING AFGHANISTAN BUT OFFERED NEXT TO NO CONCRETE EVIDENCE TO BACK HIS ACCUSATIONS. SHOULD COUNTRIES GO TO WAR ON NO EVIDENCE?

7. THE TALIBAN WAS CLEARLY REPRESSIVE AND GUILTY OF TREMENDOUS HUMAN-RIGHTS VIOLATIONS, ESPECIALLY AGAINST THE WOMEN OF AFGHANISTAN. BUT ISN'T BOMBING THE CIVILIAN POPULATION ALSO A VIOLATION OF THEIR RIGHTS?

8. BY 2001, AFTER DECADES OF CIVIL WAR, AFGHANISTAN WAS DEVASTATED. WHY WOULD ANYONE WAGE A PROLONGED WAR AGAINST A COUNTRY THAT'S ALREADY BEEN DESTROYED?

DESPITE THESE AND OTHER OBJECTIONS, AND DESPITE THE INTEMPERATE RHETORIC COMING OUT OF WASHINGTON, MOST WESTERN COUNTRIES JOINED THE GLOBAL WAR ON TERRORISM—AT LEAST AT FIRST. GREAT BRITAIN COMMITTED MILITARY ASSISTANCE. EVEN COUNTRIES TRADITIONALLY OPPOSED TO U.S. INTERVENTIONISM OFFERED UNCONDITIONAL SUPPORT FOR BUSH'S POLICIES. THE WORLD WAS AT HIS FEET.

The war on terrorism is the struggle of freedom against barbarism.

Or maybe barbarism against barbarism.

We have to finish off the terrorists. Skin them alive and rip out their fingernails!

Don't freak out on me. Here, let me give you an executive-strength tranquilizer.

Is it good for business?

It's fantastic.

And while we wait for it to take effect, let's see just how effective it is to fight barbarism with barbarism.

21. THE TERRORISM OF WAR

ON OCTOBER 7, 2001, THE U.S. STARTED BOMBING AFGHANISTAN. THE CAMPAIGN, KNOWN AS "OPERATION ENDURING FREEDOM," WOULD LAST FOR SEVERAL MONTHS.

THREE MONTHS INTO THE WAR, THE BRITISH PRESS PLACED THE NUMBER OF CIVILIAN DEATHS AT 500, BUT A U.S. PROFESSOR CALCULATED FROM LOCAL AND EUROPEAN PRESS REPORTS THAT SOME 3,500 CIVILIANS HAD DIED. BY JANUARY 2002, THE NUMBER HAD SURPASSED 5,500.

WASHINGTON CLAIMS THAT THE WAR ON TERROR IS A WAR TO PROTECT LIFE. AFTER THE FIRST BOMBINGS, A HIGH-RANKING PENTAGON OFFICIAL DECLARED:

BUT PERHAPS WHAT WAS REALLY RIDICULOUS WAS THE IDEA THAT THIS WAS A HUMANITARIAN WAR.

AS SOON AS WASHINGTON LAUNCHED ITS CAMPAIGN OF "SELECTIVE" BOMBING (USING SO-CALLED SMART BOMBS), PEOPLE WERE AFRAID OF HOW THE FUNDAMENTALISTS MIGHT RESPOND. WHEN LETTERS LACED WITH DEADLY ANTHRAX SPORES APPEARED IN THE U.S., PEOPLE PANICKED.

IN AFGHANISTAN, BUSH LENT SUPPORT TO THE NORTHERN ALLIANCE, A GROUP WITH A CRIMINAL RECORD AS BAD AS THE TALIBAN'S, THUS PROVING THAT THIS WAR HAD LITTLE TO DO WITH PRINCIPLE. WHILE THE U.S. MEDIA PROVIDED WIDESPREAD COVERAGE OF TALIBAN ATROCITIES, THOSE COMMITTED BY THE NORTHERN ALLIANCE WERE BARELY MENTIONED.

FIND THE DIFFERENCES!

U.S. ALLY IN AFGHANISTAN

U.S. ENEMY N AFGHANISTAN

ANSWER: LET US KNOW IF YOU FIND ANY AT ALL!

BESIDES, JUST AS BUSH HAD PROMISED, WASHINGTON KEPT A TIGHT LID ON INFORMATION AND MANIPULATED WHAT WAS PASSED TO THE PRESS.

You can't call me a liar, 'cause I told you up front I was going to fool you.

THE WESTERN MEDIA BROADCAST A VIDEO (AUTHENTICITY NEVER VERI-FIED) OF BIN LADEN PRAISING THE SEPTEMBER 11 ATTACKS AND CLAIMING HE KNEW OF THEM BEFOREHAND. BY DECEMBER 2001, WASHINGTON'S ALLIES HAD SUCCESSFULLY REPLACED THE TALIBAN. AT THAT POINT ANOTHER VIDEO WAS BROADCAST, THIS TIME SHOWING BIN LADEN CALLING FOR WAR AGAINST THE U.S.

THE BUSH REGIME CONSIDERED THAT THE WAR WAS FAR FROM OVER AND INSISTED IT WOULD CONTINUE MILITARY INTER-VENTIONS ANYWHERE IN THE WORLD IT DEEMED NECESSARY. THERE ARE INDICATIONS, HOWEVER, THAT THIS NEW U.S. DOCTRINE HAS GOALS FAR BEYOND THE DECLARED ONES OF FIGHTING TERRORISM.

165

22. HOW TO MAKE A BIG MESS GLOBAL

SOME ANALYSTS HAVE SUGGESTED THAT THE WAR ON TERRORISM PROVIDED WASHINGTON WITH A JUSTIFICATION TO REASSERT ITS POWER, PARTICULARLY ITS MILITARY POWER, IN THE MIDDLE EAST AND AROUND THE WORLD. AND WHEN WASHINGTON SNEEZES, THE WORLD CATCHES COLD—AND SHIVERS WITH THE THREAT OF WAR.

WITH THE GLOBALIZED ECONOMY IN CRISIS, WASHINGTON MUST PREVENT COUNTRIES FROM BLOCKING THE MULTINATIONALS' ACCESS TO KEY NATURAL RESOURCES. THAT'S WHERE WAR COMES IN HANDY.

THE U.S. IS FAR AND AWAY THE WORLD'S LARGEST CONSUMER OF OIL. DEPLETED DOMESTIC SUPPLIES AND GROWING DEMAND HAS LED IT TO DEPEND ON FOREIGN SUPPLIERS. ONE POTENTIAL SUPPLIER IS KAZAKHSTAN, WHICH HAS VAST UNTAPPED RESERVES. BUT TO GET THE OIL OUT OF KAZAKHSTAN YOU NEED A PIPELINE. AND UNLESS YOU WANT TO PIPE THAT OIL THROUGH RUSSIA, THE PIPELINE NEEDS TO GO THROUGH . . . AFGHANISTAN!

AND, OF COURSE, THERE ARE OTHER COUNTRIES IN THE REGION WITH SIMI-LARLY TEMPTING RESERVES OF BLACK GOLD . . .

FURTHERMORE, TO GET OUT OF A RECESSION, CAPITALIST COUNTRIES—PARTICULARLY THE UNITED STATES—HAVE ALWAYS REVVED UP THEIR WAR MACHINES. GIVEN THE SEVERITY OF THE 2001 ECONOMIC CRISIS, THE TOP INDUSTRIALIZED NATIONS HAD A CLEAR INTEREST IN PROLONGING THE WAR ... FOR AS LONG AS IT MIGHT TAKE TO REVIVE THE ECONOMY.

Long Live Freedom!

Freedom of Enterprise!

Especially the enterprise of making arms!

EL FISGON.

Bush's hawkish approach may have been inspired by the U.S. weapons manufacturers.

And more than a few European companies profit, too!

Drawings: Grandville (Jean Gerard)

WAR IS STILL THE MOST PROFITABLE ENTERPRISE AROUND. JUST DAYS AFTER SEPTEMBER 11, WHILE THE STOCK MARKETS WERE IN DISARRAY, ARMS MANUFACTURERS WERE REPORTING SURGES IN ORDERS.

BY KEEPING THE COUNTRY ON A CONSTANT WAR FOOTING, WASHINGTON IS ABLE TO CONTINUE SPOON-FEEDING THE ARMS INDUSTRY. OF COURSE THE PROBLEM IS THAT SOONER OR LATER THESE WEAPONS AND WAR TECHNOLOGIES GET USED ...

AND ALL THIS AT A TIME WHEN OTHERWISE THE THREAT OF WAR IS RELATIVELY LOW—AT LEAST AMONG THE INDUSTRIALIZED NATIONS. ONE REASON FOR THIS IS THAT THE U.S. IS NOW THE ONLY SUPERPOWER ON THE GLOBE—WHICH IS ALSO A REASON WHY NO ONE CAN STOP IT FROM IMPOSING ITS WILL (AND THE WILL OF ITS MULTINATIONALS) ON THE ENTIRE WORLD.

FREE MARKET DICTATORSHIP DOES NOT BROOK ANY DISSENT. IN APRIL 2002, AFTER THE POPULIST (THOUGH NOT ALWAYS POPULAR) VENEZUELAN LEADER HUGO CHÁVEZ ATTEMPTED TO SET HIS OWN POLICY REGARDING THE COUNTRY'S OIL, THE U.S. SUPPORTED A COUP TO TOPPLE HIS REGIME. A BUSINESSMAN WAS PROCLAIMED PRESIDENT AND THE VENEZUELAN CONGRESS WAS DISSOLVED.

THE COUP ATTEMPT WAS FRUSTRATED BY A POPULAR INSURRECTION AND ARMY SUPPORT FOR CHÁVEZ. BUT WASHINGTON KEPT THE PRESSURE ON HIM TO TOE THE NEOLIBERAL LINE.

IN ISRAEL, THE GOVERNMENT HARDENED ITS STANCE AGAINST THE PALESTINIANS, AND A NEW INTIFADA ENSUED, WITH TERRORISTS LAUNCHING DEADLY SUICIDE ATTACKS AGAINST ISRAELI CITIZENS. ARIEL SHARON'S GOVERNMENT RESPONDED WITH MORE VIOLENCE.

FROM THE BEGINNING OF THIS INTIFADA THROUGH MARCH 2002, OVER A THOUSAND PALESTINIANS AND MORE THAN 300 ISRAELIS HAD BEEN KILLED.

SHARON LAUNCHED AN OFFENSIVE AGAINST THE PALESTINIAN AUTHORITY, LED BY YASSER ARAFAT. WHEN THE ISRAELI ARMY INVADED THE GAZA STRIP AND THE CITY OF RAMALLAH. DOZENS WERE KILLED, HUNDREDS WOUNDED, AND THOUSANDS ARRESTED, FURTHER FUELING THE VICIOUS CYCLE.

MOST OF EUROPE CONDEMNED SHARON'S OFFENSIVE, AS DID UN OBSERVERS AND MANY ISRAELI INTELLECTUALS AND PACIFISTS. EVEN SOME ISRAELI SOLDIERS OPPOSED THE INVASION. BUT WASHINGTON SUPPORTED SHARON, ALMOST AS IF THE OBJECT OF ITS POLICY WAS TO PERPETUATE THE CONFLICT.

MEANWHILE, GEORGE W. BUSH'S ADMINISTRATION BEGAN SPEAKING OPENLY OF ITS PLAN TO INVADE IRAQ. THE FORMAL PRETEXT WAS THAT SADDAM HUSSEIN POSED A THREAT TO THE WORLD, THAT HE POSSESSED WEAPONS OF MASS DESTRUCTION, AND THAT HE HAD A HISTORY OF HUMAN RIGHTS VIOLATIONS.

We've got a dangerous madman over there in Iraq—and he's armed!

EL FISGON.

SADDAM HUSSEIN WAS UNQUESTIONABLY A TYRANT GUILTY OF THE WORST HUMAN RIGHTS VIOLATIONS—MOST OF WHICH HE HAD COMMITTED BACK WHEN HE ENJOYED THE SUPPORT OF THE WEST. U.S. COMPANIES HAD ALSO SOLD HIM BIOLOGICAL AGENTS, SUCH AS ANTHRAX. BY 2002, HOWEVER, IRAQ HAD BEEN DEVASTATED BY YEARS OF WAR AND SANCTIONS AND CLEARLY POSED NO THREAT TO THE WORLD. WHAT IRAQ DID HAVE WAS HUGE RESERVES OF OIL...

IN 2003, THE BUSH ADMINISTRATION PREPARED FOR INVASION, DESPITE OPPOSITION FROM MUCH OF THE WORLD. HUGE PEACE DEMONSTRATIONS ERUPTED ACROSS THE PLANET, AND DESPITE HIS STRONG-ARM TACTICS, BUSH ONLY WON THE SUPPORT OF A FEW NATIONS, NOTABLY THE UK, AND FAILED TO OBTAIN THE BLESSING OF THE UN. BUT THAT DIDN'T STOP HIM . . .

BUSH ACTED LIKE AN EMPEROR, UNACCOUNTABLE TO ANYONE.

ON MARCH 19, DOZENS OF HUGE BOMBS AND CRUISE MISSILES RAINED DOWN ON THE IRAQI CAPITAL OF BAGHDAD. CONTRARY TO WASHINGTON'S PROPAGANDA, THE IRAQIS DID NOT RECEIVE THEIR "LIBERATORS" WITH OPEN ARMS. THE MAJOR FIGHTING WAS SOON OVER, BUT MILLIONS OF INNOCENT CIVILIANS SUFFERED THE HORRORS OF WAR.

WITHIN A FEW WEEKS, MORE THAN 9,000 BOMBS AND MISSILES HAD BEEN DROPPED ON IRAQ. THE UN CALLED FOR HELP TO ADDRESS THE HUMANITARIAN DISASTER.

SADDAM HUSSEIN FLED AND THE IRAQI ARMY PUT UP LITTLE RESISTANCE. BY APRIL 10, THE INVADERS HAD TAKEN BAGHDAD, BUT THEY TURNED UP NO SIGN OF WEAPONS OF MASS DESTRUCTION.

HANS BLIX, THE CHIEF WEAPONS INSPECTOR FOR THE UN, INSISTED THAT THE CLAIMS OF BUSH AND BRITISH PRIME MINISTER TONY BLAIR REGARDING IRAQ'S ARSENAL DID NOT SQUARE WITH HIS FINDINGS.

NO SOONER HAD THEY OCCUPIED IRAQ, BUT THE U.S. AND UK RUSHED TO PROTECT WHAT THEY WERE MOST INTERESTED IN: THE OIL FIELDS, THE OIL MINISTRY, AND THE INTERIOR MINISTRY, WHERE FILES WERE KEPT ON IRAQI CITIZENS. BUT THEY DID NOTHING TO STOP LOOTERS FROM DESTROYING PRICELESS LIBRARIES AND MUSEUMS. MUCH OF IRAQ'S HISTORY AND MANY OF ITS ANCIENT WORKS OF ART WERE DEMOLISHED.

THE U.S. AND UK INSTALLED AN INTERIM MILITARY GOVERNMENT, WHICH THEY PROMISED WOULD BE TEMPORARY (AT LEAST TWO YEARS), AND BEGAN PUTTING TOGETHER A WESTERN-FRIENDLY CIVILIAN REGIME. THEIR FIRST CHOICE TO LEAD IT WAS AHMED CHALABI, A BUSINESSMAN IMPLICATED IN MILLION-DOLLAR SWINDLES.

WHEN THE MAJORITY SHIITE POPULATION PROTESTED AGAINST THE OCCUPY-ING FORCES, WASHINGTON CLAIMED IRAN WAS BEHIND IT. AND THEY ACCUSED SYRIA OF HAVING CHEMICAL WEAPONS . . . SIGNS THAT SUGGEST OTHER INVASIONS MAY BE JUST AROUND THE CORNER.

THE EMPIRE OF FREE TRADE SEEMS TO REQUIRE BOTH.

WHAT'S MORE, WAR PROVIDES AN EXCELLENT EXCUSE FOR RESTRICTING CERTAIN RIGHTS, SUCH AS FREEDOM OF EXPRESSION AND FREEDOM OF THE PRESS. AND IN TIMES OF CRISIS, SUCH AS 2001, GOVERNMENTS FEEL OBLIGED TO CONTROL PUBLIC OPINION.

THIS EXPLAINS THE BUSH ADMINISTRATION'S ATTEMPTS AT CENSORSHIP DURING THE INVASION OF AFGHANISTAN.

ONE DOCUMENT FROM THE U.S. NATIONAL SECURITY COUNCIL FOCUSES ON THE GOVERNABILITY OF VARIOUS COUNTRIES IN THE NEAR FUTURE.

A war against an enemy as vague as international terrorism, which extends beyond clearly defined national borders . . .

. . . is the ideal pretext for stamping out the anti-globalization movement . . .

. . . or any nationalist stirrings.

Nothing justifies terrorism.

But perhaps terrorism flourishes more easily in a world where injustice is rampant, humiliation widespread, and future prospects dim.

AND IT'S CLEAR THAT THE NEOLIBERAL SYSTEM GENERATES EXACTLY SUCH CONDITIONS. REMEMBER ARGENTINA.

ARGENTINA PRIVATIZED ITS ECONOMY, OPENED ITS MARKETS, AND GAVE BIG BUSINESS THE FREEDOM TO DO WHAT IT PLEASED. THEN, IN 1999 THE ECONOMY COLLAPSED. THE RICH RAN AWAY WITH THEIR MONEY WHILE THE GOVERNMENT WHISTLED AND LOOKED THE OTHER WAY. ONCE ALL THAT CASH WAS SAFELY STASHED ABROAD, PRESIDENT DE LA RÚA IMPLEMENTED THE STANDARD IMF SHOCK THERAPY. HE SLASHED WAGES, SUSPENDED PENSION PAYMENTS, AND FROZE PERSONAL BANK ACCOUNTS. PEOPLE TOOK TO THE STREETS—INCLUDING THE MIDDLE CLASS. THERE WAS LOOTING, RIOTING, AND REPRESSION. TWENTY-FIVE PEOPLE DIED.

MARTIAL LAW WAS DECLARED, DE LA RÚA RESIGNED, AND AN INTERIM PRES-IDENT DECLARED A MORATORIUM ON DEBT PAYMENTS. THE COUNTRY WENT THROUGH FIVE PRESIDENTS IN LESS THAN TWO WEEKS.

WASHINGTON AND WALL STREET, HOWEVER, REMAINED UNMOVED. EVEN AS ARGENTINA COLLAPSED, THE U.S. AND THE IMF CONTINUED LEANING ON THE COUNTRY TO STICK WITH THE NEOLIBERAL PROGRAM.

THAT'S HOW THE POWERFUL TREATED THE MOST LOYAL FOLLOWER OF IMF AND WORLD BANK POLICY.

BY 2001 ARGENTINA WAS BANKRUPT. BETWEEN MARCH AND DECEMBER OF THAT YEAR $18 BILLION FLED THE COUNTRY. FORTY PERCENT OF THE POPULATION—SOME 14.5 MILLION PEOPLE—HAD FALLEN INTO POVERTY.

SINCE OTHER LATIN AMERICAN ECONOMIES WERE ALSO FOLLOWING THE DICTATES OF THE IMF AND THE WORLD BANK, ANALYSTS FEARED THAT THEY, TOO, WOULD COLLAPSE. AND THAT WOULD LEAD TO UNPRECEDENTED CHAOS, ESPECIALLY SINCE AT THE BEGINNING OF THE 21st CENTURY WORKING PEOPLE WERE NOW COMPLETELY DEFENSELESS AGAINST UNCHECKED MARKET GREED.

AT LEAST IN THE PAST,
PEOPLE WERE ABLE TO
DEFEND THEMSELVES
THROUGH LABOR UNIONS
OR NATIONAL RESISTANCE
MOVEMENTS.

POPULAR RESISTANCE OF THIS SORT, WHICH USHERED IN SOCIALISM AND THE
WELFARE STATE, HAD MANAGED TO CHECK THE RAPACITY OF CAPITALISM. BUT
NO LONGER.

THE U.S. IS GLOBALIZATION'S CHIEF ADVOCATE, AS WELL AS ITS MAJOR BENE-
FICIARY. IT IS ALSO THE MIGHTIEST MILITARY POWER IN THE WORLD. THE
THREAT OF WAR ALLOWS WASHINGTON TO KEEP THE NEOLIBERAL SYSTEM IN
PLACE AND MAINTAIN AMERICAN CONTROL OVER THE REST OF THE WORLD.

IN THIS RESPECT, THE AMERICAN WAR AGAINST INTERNATIONAL TERRORISM,
BUSH'S BELLICOSE RHETORIC, AND THE INVASIONS OF AFGHANISTAN AND
IRAQ ARE ALL PART OF THE RECOLONIZATION OF THE THIRD WORLD.

IN THE CURRENT PHASE, POOR COUNTRIES ARE CAUGHT BETWEEN THE THREAT OF WAR AND THE THREAT OF SOCIAL EXPLOSION, AND POOR PEOPLE ARE AT THE MERCY OF A VORACIOUS FREE-MARKET SYSTEM AND A WARRIOR EMPIRE THAT WILL STOP AT NOTHING TO PROTECT ITS PRIVILEGED POSITION.

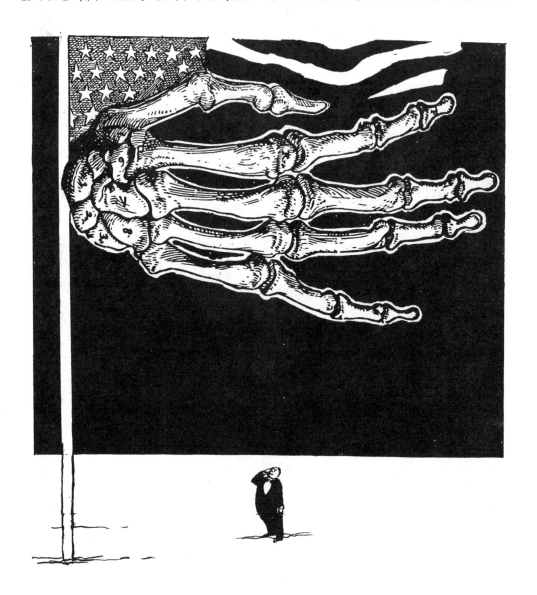

TODAY MORE THAN EVER PEOPLE NEED TO GET ORGANIZED, BECAUSE IF WE DON'T DEFEND OURSELVES, WE WILL BE CRUSHED.

23. A PROGRAM OF ACTION

THE FREE-TRADE EMPIRE OWES ITS POWER TO TWO BASIC FACTORS:

1. The power of capital and the ability of multinational corporations to exploit the technological revolution.

2. The historical failure of leftist programs, including the corruption of social democratic and national-populist movements, and the horrors of communist regimes.

TRADITIONAL LEFTIST ORGANIZATIONS NEED TO CHANGE. THEY NEED TO ENGAGE IN MORE DEBATE, EXPAND THEIR APPROACH, AND FIND A WAY TO REACH OUT TO A BROAD PUBLIC. TODAY'S ACTIVISTS KNOW THAT A GLOBALIZED WORLD REQUIRES A NEW PLAN OF ACTION.

1. GLOBAL ORGANIZATIONS OF WORKERS AND NETWORKS OF SOLIDARITY.

THE NEOLIBERAL MODEL IS LIMPING ALONG FROM ONE CRISIS TO THE NEXT, AND DISCONTENT IS RISING DAILY.

BUT UNLESS WE DEVELOP A CLEAR PLATFORM OF STRUGGLE AGAINST THE STATUS QUO, IT COULD DRAG ON FOR YEARS.

2. AN INTERNATIONAL PEACE MOVEMENT AGAINST FREE-TRADE IMPERIALISM.

SINCE UNFETTERED FREE TRADE REQUIRES FREQUENT WARS, WE MUST WAGE PEACE. NO MORE WARS. NO MORE U.S. ARMED INTERVENTIONS.

EVERY REGIONAL STRUGGLE, IF IT IS TO SURVIVE AND TRIUMPH, MUST BE LINKED WITH THIS GLOBAL PEACE MOVEMENT.

3. TECHNOLOGY IN THE SERVICE OF PEACE AND DEVELOPMENT.

TODAY TECHNOLOGY IS ONE OF THE CHIEF WEAPONS OF THE FREE-TRADE EMPIRE. WE MUST USE IT TO DEFEND AGAINST EXPLOITATION.

ONE FORM OF TECHNOLOGY THAT THE NEOLIBERALS DON'T UNDERSTAND IS ... SOLIDARITY.

4. AN END TO LAWS THAT DISCRIMINATE AGAINST MIGRANT WORKERS.

NEOLIBERALISM PREACHES OPEN BORDERS FOR TRADE BUT NOT FOR PEOPLE.

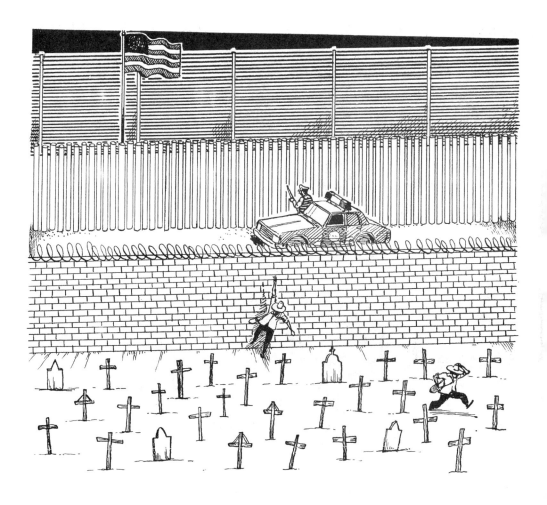

IT IS INTOLERABLE THAT CAPITAL AND COMMODITIES HAVE MORE RIGHTS THAN HUMAN BEINGS.

5. DEVELOPMENT-FRIENDLY INTERNATIONAL TRADE AGREEMENTS.

FREE TRADE OBLIGES POOR COUNTRIES TO NEGOTIATE WITH RICH ONES AS IF THEY WERE ON THE SAME FOOTING. THIS IS A GREAT INJUSTICE. POOR REGIONS NEED PROTECTION FROM CORPORATE GREED. TRADE AGREEMENTS NEED TO BENEFIT THE MAJORITY.

THE EUROPEAN COMMUNITY IS A BETTER MODEL. POORER REGIONS AND SECTORS OF THE ECONOMY NEED TO BE SUBSIDIZED, NOT DESTROYED—ESPECIALLY AGRICULTURE, WHICH IS ALREADY TEETERING ON THE EDGE.

6. STRICT REGULATION OF CAPITAL AND EXECUTIVE ACCOUNTABILITY.

BUSINESSES MUST NOT BE ALLOWED TO GO ON PERPETRATING MULTI-BILLION-DOLLAR SCAMS. SEVERE PUNISHMENTS SHOULD BE METED OUT TO CORPORATE CRIMINALS.

Mexico: Financial Elites Pull Spectacular Fraud. Government Plays Along.

Argentina: Financial Elites Pull Spectacular Fraud. Government Plays Along.

USA: Financial Elites Pull Spectacular Fraud. Government Plays Along.

YEAH!

Actually, these mega-ripoffs aren't news ... They're just business as usual.

SUCH CRIMES HAVE BROUGHT SUFFERING AND DEATH TO MILLIONS. THE PERPETRATORS SHOULD BE TRIED FOR CRIMES AGAINST HUMANITY IN THE INTERNATIONAL CRIMINAL COURT.

7. NO MORE PRIVATIZATIONS.

PUBLIC ASSETS ARE BETTER THAN PRIVATE ONES. PRIVATIZATION PUTS THE WEALTH OF NATIONS, ACCUMULATED OVER YEARS OF WORK AND SACRIFICE, IN THE HANDS OF A FEW POWERFUL OWNERS—MOST OF WHOM WOULDN'T THINK TWICE ABOUT ROBBING THEIR OWN COUNTRY.

MOREOVER, WHEN MULTINATIONAL CORPORATIONS ACQUIRE A COUNTRY'S STRATEGIC ENTERPRISES, THEY USE THEM AS LEVERAGE TO IMPOSE THEIR WILL ON THE GOVERNMENT.

8. AN IMMEDIATE MORATORIUM ON THIRD WORLD DEBT.

THERE IS NO WAY THESE DEBTS CAN BE PAID OFF, ALTHOUGH IN FACT THEY HAVE BEEN PAID SEVERAL TIMES OVER. MEXICO ALONE HAS PAID WHAT IT BORROWED IN THE 1970s SEVEN TIMES OVER—YET NOW IT OWES MORE THAN EVER.

THE FOREIGN DEBT IS A TOOL WHICH POWERFUL CORPORATIONS AND NATIONS USE TO DRAIN THE WEALTH OF SMALLER COUNTRIES AND MANIPULATE THEIR GOVERNMENTS.

ACKNOWLEDGMENTS

Many thanks to Adolfo Gilly, Roberto González, Guillermo Almeyra, Alma Muñoz, Carlos Fernández Vega, Jim Cason, David Brooks, and Juan Antonio Zuñiaga for providing me with background information.

I am also grateful to my colleagues Rius, Helguera, and José Hernández for their comments, and for allowing me to reproduce some of their own cartoons.

My thanks to Mark Fried for his translation, Philip Boehm for his help in preparing the English edition, and my friends at Metropolitan Books—Sara Bershtel, Riva Hocherman, Shara Kay, John Candell, and Paula Szafranski. For having brought my work to America, I owe special thanks to Tom Engelhardt and Adam Hochschild.

The vast majority of the cartoons in this book originally appeared in *La Jornada*, and several in *Milenio Semanal* and *El Chamuco*.

ABOUT THE AUTHOR

EL FISGÓN is Mexico's leading political cartoonist, author of seven cartoon books, cofounder of two satirical magazines, and an illustrator of
children's books. A winner of Mexico's National Journalism Prize, he
lives in Mexico City.

THE AMERICAN EMPIRE PROJECT

In an era of unprecedented military strength, leaders of the United States, the global hyperpower, have increasingly embraced imperial ambitions. How did this significant shift in purpose and policy come about? And what lies down the road?

The American Empire Project is a response to the changes that have occurred in American's strategic thinking as well as in its military and economic posture. Empire, long considered an offense against America's democratic heritage, now threatens to define the relationship between our country and the rest of the world. The American Empire Project publishes books that question this development, examine the origins of U.S. imperial aspirations, analyze their ramifications at home and abroad, and discuss alternatives to this dangerous trend.

The project was conceived by Tom Engelhardt and Steve Fraser, editors who are themselves historians and writers. Published by Metropolitan Books, an imprint of Henry Holt and Company, its debut volumes were *Hegemony or Survival* by Noam Chomsky and *The Sorrows of Empire* by Chalmers Johnson.

For more information about the American Empire Project and for a list of forthcoming titles, please visit www.americanempireproject.com.